Introduction to Canva

Setting up an Canva account and getting familiar with the interface

Getting familiar with the Canva interface	3
Elements tab	6
view element collection	8
Using Canva's design elements such as shapes and lines,	9
Switch shapes	10
Design tab	11
Style Tab	12
Uploading	14
Adding text and images	15
Basic Text Editing in Canva	16
Add, delete, duplicate, lock, hide and name page	18
Show Rulers and guides	19
Bleeds and margins	20
Text effects	21
Adding Drop Shadow	24
Adding Color	25
Gradients	26
add text to shapes	27
Find and replace	28

Copy style	29
Connecting lines and shapes	30
Text on line	31
Folders	32
Access designs	33
Duplicate design	34
Tables	35
Introduction to Frames	37
Introduction to Grids	38
Star a template, photo and elements	40
Choosing templates and customizing designs	41
Exporting and sharing designs	43
Collaborating with others on designs	45
Understanding File Types in Canva	48
Applying effects to photo	52
Adding outline to photos	53
Crop photo	55
Flip photo	56
Transparency	57
Lock	58
Grouping	59
Deleting	60
Duplicate Elements	61
Position: arranging elements	62
Position: Aligning elements	63

Position: placing elements and setting dimensions	65
Layers	66
Choosing templates and customizing designs	67
customizing template	68
Creating Instagram post in 5 steps	72
Creating Instagram post for Pizza	74
Animation: Text animation	76
Animation	85
Page Animation	87
Adding and editing Videos	89
draw	96
Magic Write	97
Docs	99
Magic Edit	101
Magic Media	103
keyboard shortcuts	104
Useful Links	106

INTRODUCTION TO CANVA
Its Purpose And Key Features

Canva is an online graphic design platform that allows users to create stunning designs with ease, even without prior design experience. It is a user-friendly tool that offers a wide range of templates, images, and design elements, making it a great option for both personal and professional use.

PURPOSE OF CANVA

Canva was created with the goal of making design accessible to everyone, regardless of their design skills or experience. The platform provides an easy-to-use interface, intuitive drag-and-drop features, and a large library of design elements to help users create professional-looking designs in no time.

KEY FEATURES OF CANVA

- **User-friendly interface:** Canva has a simple and intuitive interface that makes it easy to navigate and use.
- **Wide range of templates:** Canva offers a vast library of templates for various design needs, such as social media graphics, presentations, invitations, and more.
- **Customization options:** Users can customize templates or create their designs from scratch using Canva's design elements, such as images, graphics, text, and more.
- **Large design element library:** Canva has a large library of design elements, including icons, shapes, lines, and more, that users can use to enhance their designs.
- **Effects and filters:** Canva offers a variety of effects and filters that can be applied to designs to enhance their appearance and make them stand out.
- **Collaboration and sharing:** Canva allows users to collaborate with others on designs and easily share their designs through various platforms, including social media, email, and more.

In summary, Canva is a powerful and user-friendly design platform that makes it easy for anyone to create professional-looking designs. Whether you are looking to create social media graphics, presentations, invitations, or any other type of design, Canva has everything you need to get started.

SETTING UP AN CANVA ACCOUNT AND GETTING FAMILIAR WITH THE INTERFACE

In this chapter, I will walk you through the process of setting up a Canva account and getting familiar with the platform's interface.

SETTING UP A CANVA ACCOUNT

Visit the Canva website at **www.canva.com**

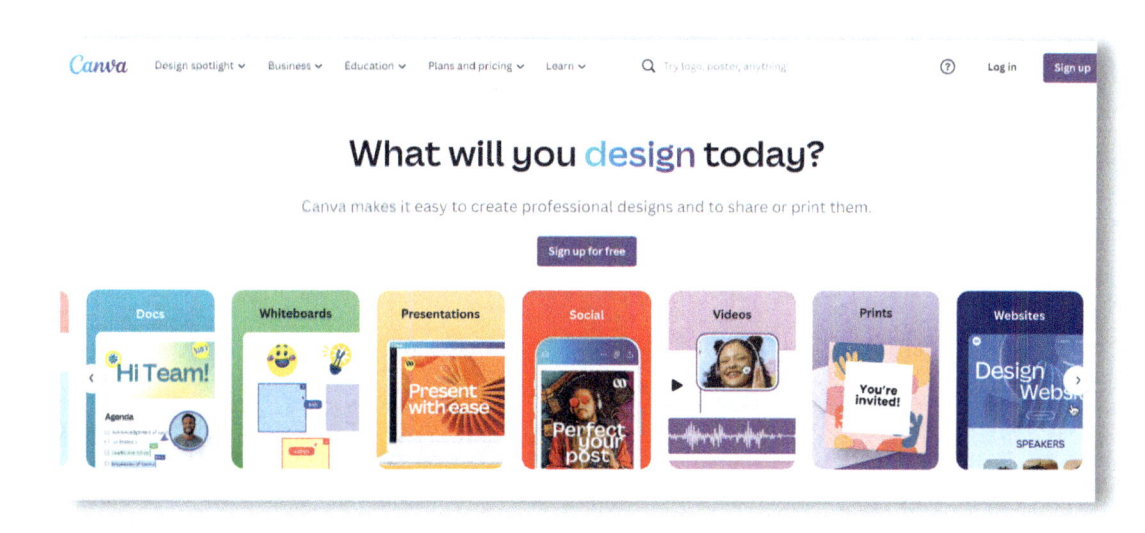

Click on the "**Sign Up**" button in the top right corner of the screen. You can sign up with Google account, Facebook, Email.

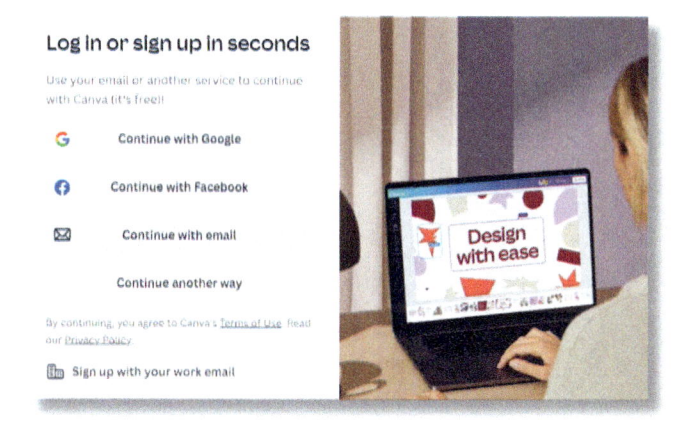

- Enter your email address and create a password.
- Fill out the required information.
- Verify your email address by clicking on the verification link sent to your email.

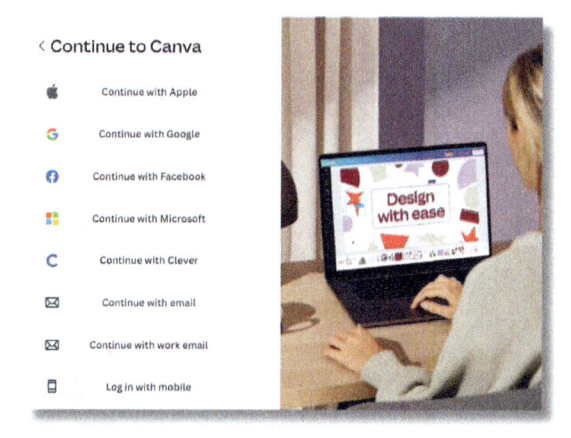

Or there are many ways as well when you click on other ways

That's it you are ready to use Canva for FREE

2

GETTING FAMILIAR WITH THE CANVA INTERFACE

Once you have set up your Canva account, you will be taken to the Canva dashboard. This is the main interface for the platform and is where you will access all of your designs and templates.

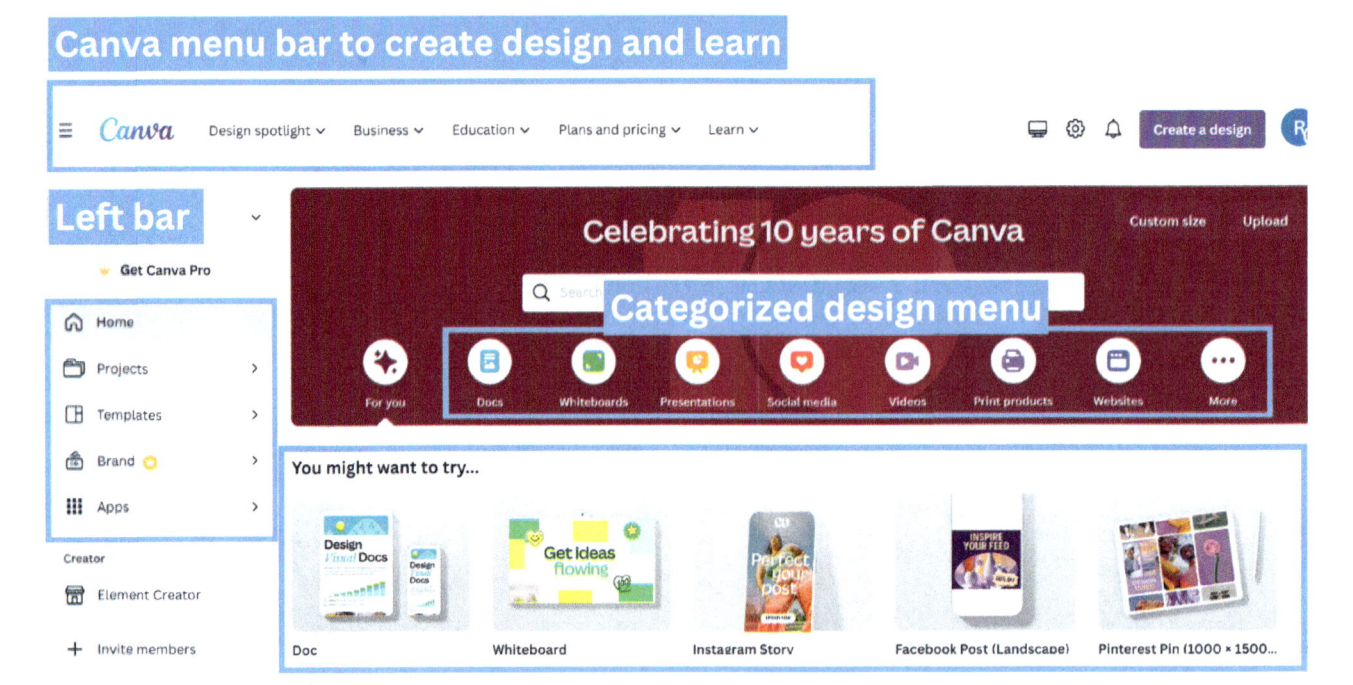

GETTING FAMILIAR WITH THE CANVA INTERFACE

Once you have set up your Canva account, you will be taken to the Canva dashboard. This is the main interface for the platform and is where you will access all of your designs and templates.

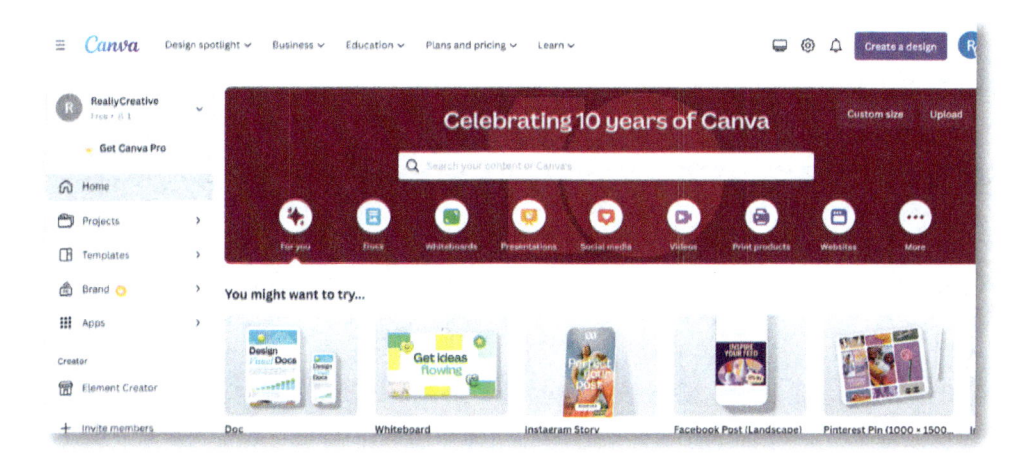

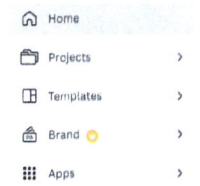

On the left-hand side of the screen, you will see a menu with various options, including "Home," "Templates," "Designs," and "Brand Kit." These options allow you to access different parts of the Canva platform.

In the center of the screen, you will see a list of your most recent designs, as well as options to create a new design or access a template. This is the central area where you'll build your design. You can add elements, text, images, and backgrounds here.

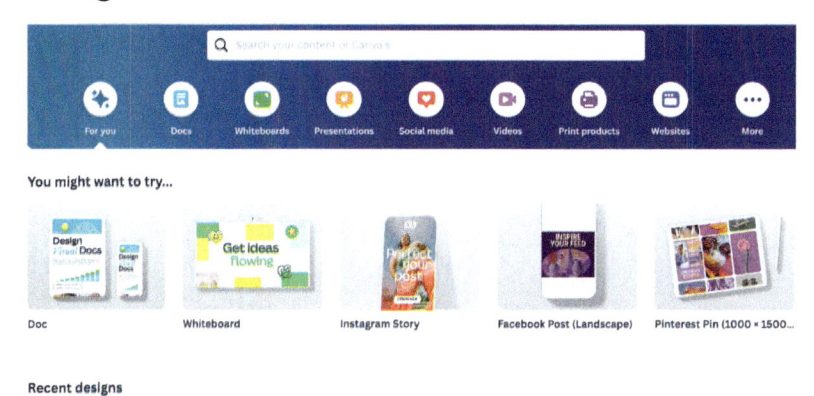

Top bar has options to save, download, resize, undo and redo

Now that you have an account and are familiar with the interface, you are ready to start creating designs with Canva.

GETTING FAMILIAR WITH THE CANVA INTERFACE

Canva has free and pro version. So how can you differentiate between them? This applies to the entire Canva interface.

Pro:
Throughout the Canva interface you will see a crown icon at the bottom Right of elements, template, audio, video, etc. This means it is PRO. You need Canva PRO for this.

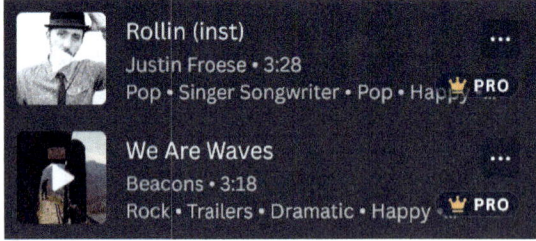

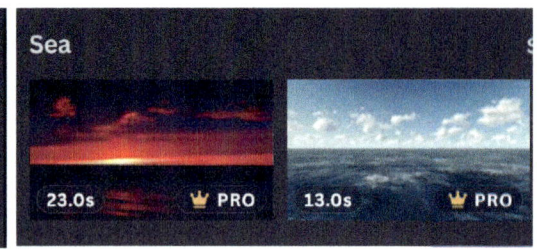

Free:
Throughout the Canva interface if you will see no icon at the bottom Right of elements, template, audio, video, etc. This means it is FREE.

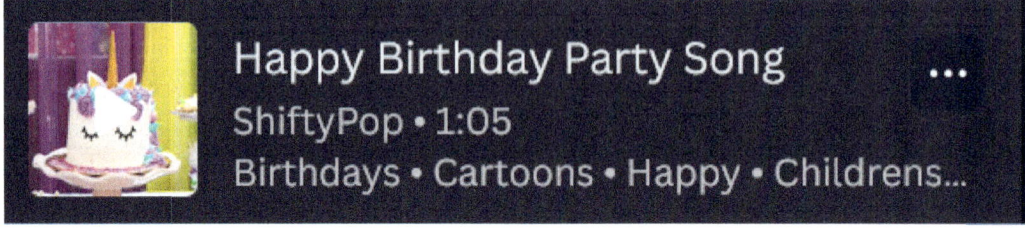

Paid
Throughout the Canva interface if you will see a Paid written icon at the bottom Right of elements, template, audio, video, etc. This means it is Paid.

ELEMENTS TAB

The 'Elements' tab in Canva is your gateway to the design wonderland. It's where you discover a rich assortment of graphics, icons, shapes, video, audio and illustrations. It can be said as the heart of Canva. You will find everything here.

Adding elements:

The elements tab is neatly divided into sections for graphics, icons, shapes, video, audio and illustrations.

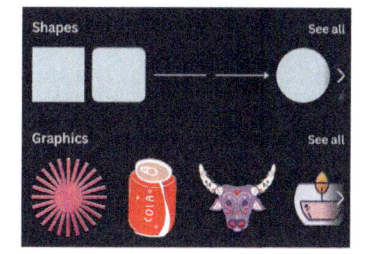

Choose Your Element: Browse through the categories, such as "Graphics," "Icons," "Photos," "Videos," "Audio," "Shapes," and more. Click on the category that suits your design needs.

Search for Specific Elements: If you have a specific element in mind, use the search bar at the top of the "Elements" tab. Type in keywords, and Canva will display relevant options.

Select and Add: Once you've found the element you want, click on it. It will be added to your design canvas.

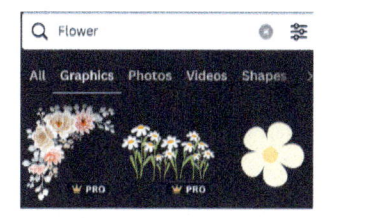

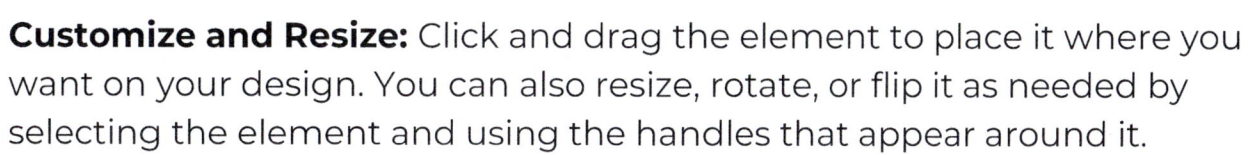

Customize and Resize: Click and drag the element to place it where you want on your design. You can also resize, rotate, or flip it as needed by selecting the element and using the handles that appear around it.

ELEMENTS TAB

Change Color: Some of the elements have options to Change colors. Click on the element and select colors from the topbar of the design

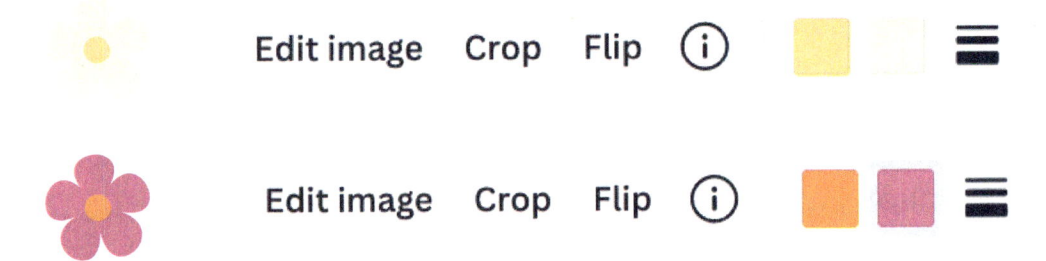

Add effects: Some of the elements have options to add effects. Click on Edit Photo from top-bar of the design and

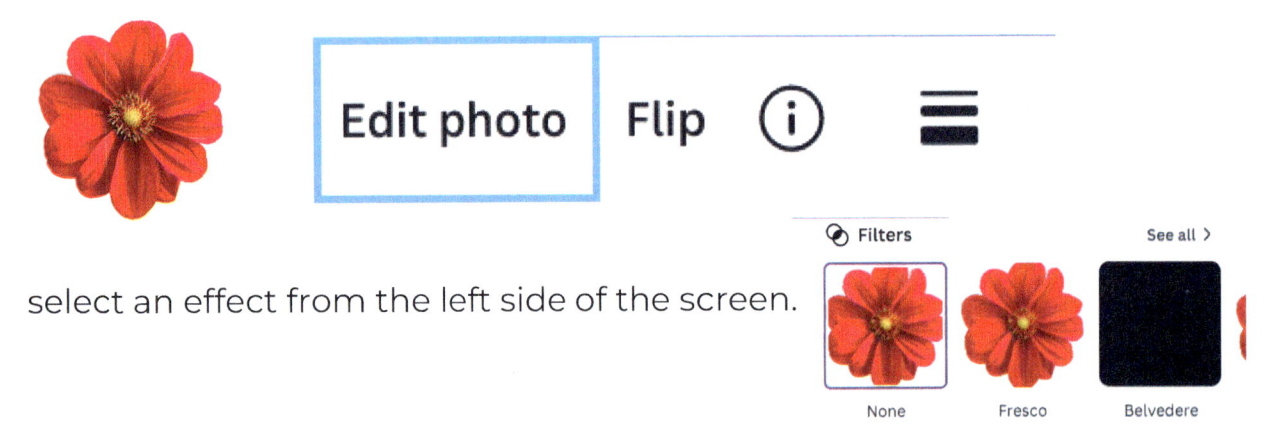

select an effect from the left side of the screen.

Delete Elements: To remove an element, select it and press the "Delete" key or use the trash can icon in the top toolbar.

Similarly, You can seamlessly incorporate audio and video elements using the dedicated "Audio" and "Video" tabs, adding depth and interactivity to your projects.

Maintaining visual structure is a breeze with the "Frames" and "Grids" options, enabling you to organize your content in a visually appealing way.

Additionally, for data-driven designs, the "Graphs" section allows you to effortlessly create and insert informative charts and graphs. Canva provides a versatile toolkit to breathe life into your designs, ensuring they are dynamic, engaging, and tailored to your specific needs.

A comprehensive exploration of these features is presented in dedicated chapters, ensuring you have in-depth guidance for each aspect.

VIEW ELEMENT COLLECTION

Elements are created by many creators. Every designer has their own style. So when we design we need cohesive designs, right? So check out the elements collection. It usually has same style elements.

Where to find elements collection.

Select the element then click on the i icon on the top bar

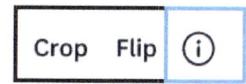

Then click on View collection

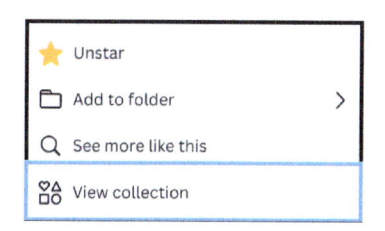

On the left pane of the screen you will see the entire collection

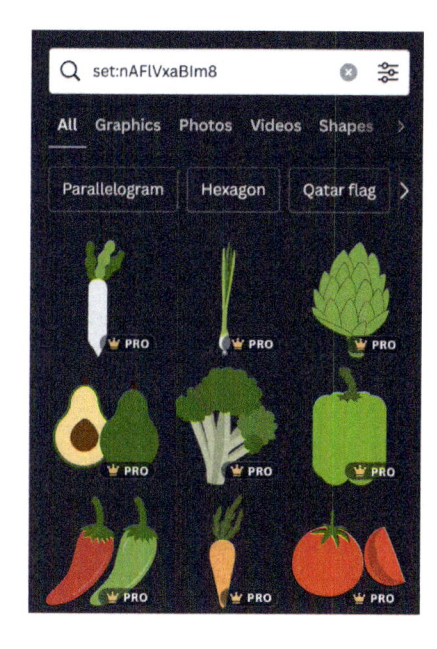

Elements collections have similar elements and makes it easy to find related and cohesive elements

8

USING CANVA DESIGN ELEMENTS SUCH AS SHAPES AND LINES,

Canva offers a variety of design elements that can be used to enhance the visual appeal of your designs. In this chapter, we will explore the process of adding shapes, lines, and icons to your designs.

Adding shapes:

To add a shape to your design,
click on the "Elements" tab
in the from the left of the screen.
Then Click on Shapes

Choose the type of shape you want to add,
such as a rectangle, circle, triangle, etc.

You can customize the shape by adjusting its size, color, and more using the options in the top bar of the design.

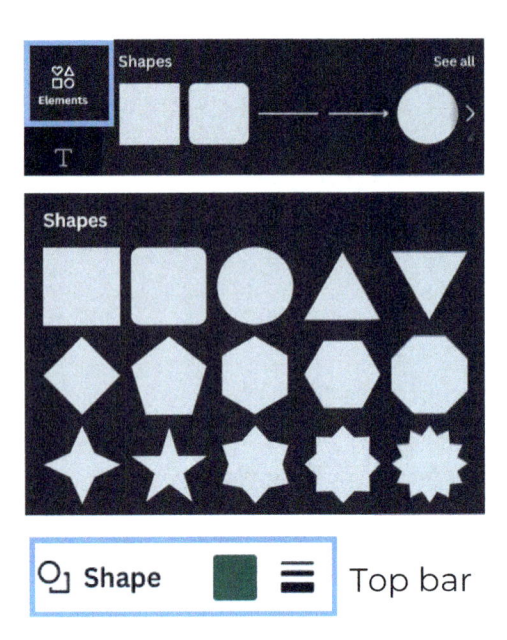

Once you have added a shape to your design, you can move, resize, and adjust it as needed.

Adding Lines:

To add a line to your design,
click on the "Elements" tab
in the from the left of the screen.
Then Click on Shapes

Choose the type of line you want to add,
such as a solid, dotted, dashed, with arrow, etc

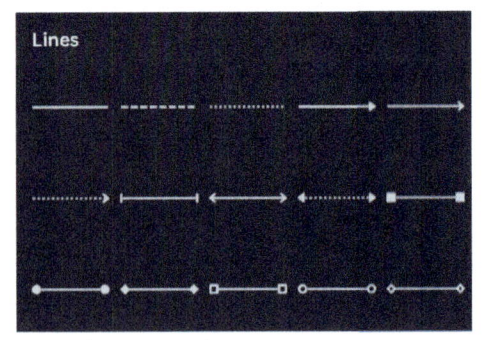

You can customize the shape by adjusting its size, color, and more using the options in the top bar of the design.

Once you have added a shape to your design, you can move, resize, and adjust it as needed.

SWITCH SHAPES

Switching shapes in Canva is a flexible way to experiment with different design elements and customize your visuals. It allows you to maintain a cohesive design while exploring a variety of shape options to best convey your message or aesthetics.

How to switch shapes:
1. Select the Shape: Click on the shape you wish to change. This will select the shape and display resizing handles around it.
2. Access the "Shapes" Option: In the top toolbar, you'll typically find a "Shapes" option. Click on it to browse through various shape options.
3. Choose a New Shape: Scroll through the available shape options and select the one you want to switch to. Click on the new shape to add it to your design canvas. Essentially, it will replace the current shape with new one shape.
4. Resize and Reposition: The new shape will be added to your canvas. You can now resize, reposition, or edit the shape to fit your design requirements.

Switching shapes in Canva is a design freedom that lets you transform and refine your visuals with ease, ensuring your creative vision comes to life seamlessly.

DESIGN TAB

Design tab is where you will find all the templates and style. Canva allows you to create designs in many ways. This is a tab where you will find templates for any design. Templates act a good starting point.

Adding Template:

Select the design tab from left side of the screen.

Here you will find templates related to the design you have selected. For example, You have created a blank Instagram Post then you will get templates related to Instagram post. However, If you are looking for some other template just type in the The Template search bar what you are looking for and you will get all the templates.

With the Design tab, Canva simplifies the process of creating a design from scratch by providing base templates.

STYLE TAB

The Style tab within Canva is your secret weapon for effortlessly adding color and font schemes to your designs.

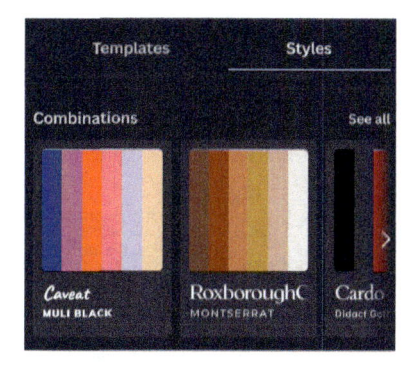

Applying predefined styles in Canva is a straightforward process that can significantly enhance the visual appeal and consistency of your designs. Here's a step-by-step guide:

1. **Open Your Design:** Begin by opening the design you want to work on in Canva.
2. **Access the Style Tab:** To apply predefined styles, navigate to the "Style" tab, typically found in the left sidebar. Click on it to access a range of pre-defined styles.
3. **Choose a Style:**
   - Color Pallets: In the "Color Palletes" section, you'll see a selection of pre-defined color palettes. Click on the one that best suits your design's mood and purpose.
   - Font sets: In the "Font Sets" section, you'll find pre-designed font pairings. Select the one that aligns with your design's typographic needs.
   - Combination: This has both Color and font pairs. You'll find pre-designed Color and font pairings. Select the one that aligns with your design.
4. **Apply the Style:**
   Once you choose a color scheme, font set, the colors and fonts will be applied to your design. Canva will automatically update the colors of text, shapes, and other elements in your project to match the selected scheme.

STYLE TAB

- Customization:
  - After applying a predefined style, you can further customize it to suit your specific design. This includes adjusting individual colors or changing font sizes and styles.

Base template

After applying Color pallets

After applying Color pallets and font set

With the Style tab, Canva simplifies the process of infusing your designs with the perfect color and font combinations.

UPLOADING

When creating a design you always need to upload your design resources such as photo, images, audio or video. Again there are many ways to upload your resources. Upload tab being one of them.

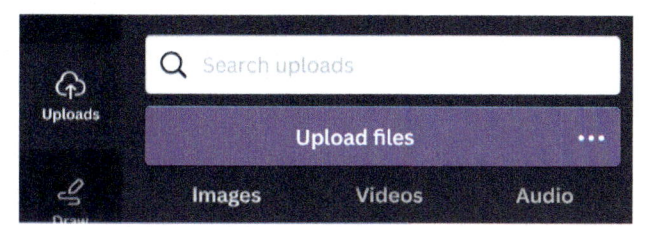

- Uploading Files:
    - In the design editor, you'll find options to upload files on the left sidebar of the screen.
    - Click on the "Upload Files" This will typically open a file uploader.
    - After selecting your files, click the "Open" button. Canva will begin uploading your files to your account. The time it takes to upload depends on the file size and your internet connection.
    - Once the files are uploaded, Canva will typically categorize them under "All Your Uploads." You can also create folders to organize your uploads for easier access in the future.
    - To use your uploaded files in your design, simply Click on them and it will be added into your design canvas. You can resize and position them as needed.

File Types you can upload in Canva
- JPEG, PNG, HEIC/HEIF, WebP images, SVG images
- Audio
- M4A, MP3, OGG, WAV, or WEBM file format
- Videos
- MOV, GIF, MP4, MPEG, MKV, or WEBM file format
- Adobe Illustrator files
- PowerPoint presentations
- PowerPoint presentations
- PDF files

By following these steps, you can easily upload your own files into Canva to create visually appealing and customized designs for various purposes.

ADDING TEXT AND IMAGES

One of the key features of Canva is the ability to add text, images, and graphics to your designs. In this chapter, we will explore the process of adding these elements to your designs.

Adding text:

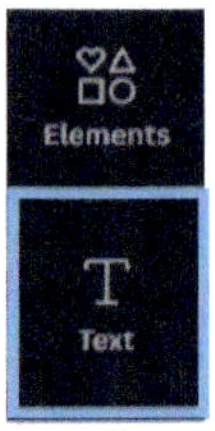

To add text to your design, click on the "Text" option in the toolbar from the left of the screen.

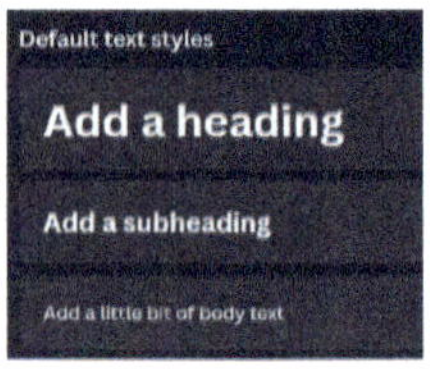

Select the type of text you want to add, such as a headline, subhead, or body text.

Type in your desired text, and use the options in the panel on the top of the screen to adjust the font, size, color, and more.

Once you have added text to your design, you can move, resize, and adjust it as needed.

Adding images:

To add an image to your design,
go to elements tab from left of the screen,
then click on photos
You can choose an image from Canva's library of millions of images,

or you can upload your own by clicking on the Upload tab from the left side of the screen.

Once you have selected an image just click on it and it will be added to your design, you can now move, resize, and adjust it as needed.

BASIC TEXT EDITING

In this chapter, we'll explore the basics of text editing in Canva. Whether you're creating a social media post, a business card, or any other type of design, text is an essential part of the design process. With Canva's text editing tools, you can easily add and customize text to your designs.

Adding Text to Your Design

To add text to your design, simply click the "Text" tab on the left-hand side of the screen and select the type of text you want to add.

You can choose from a variety of pre-designed text blocks, or you can create your own custom text by clicking the
"Add a Heading" or
"Add a Subheading" or
" add a little bit of body text" buttons.

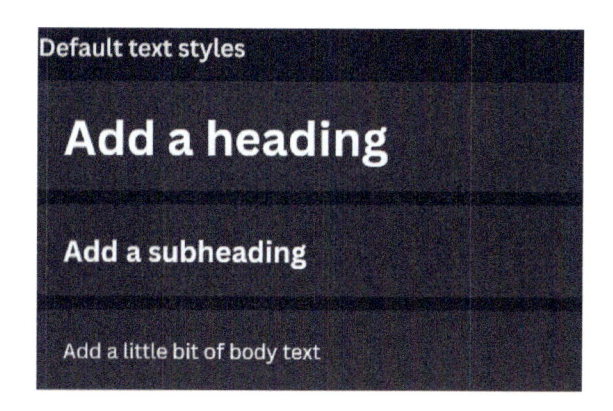

Customizing Text

Once you've added text to your design, you can customize it to fit your needs. You can change the font, size, color, and alignment of your text by using the text editing tools in the top of the canvas.

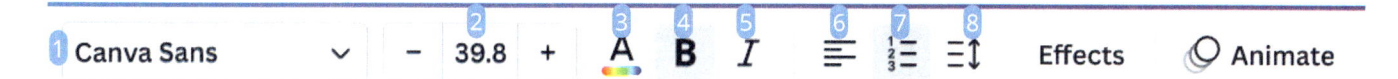

1. Fonts: You can will see the drop down list "Font" dropdown menu. Click on it to see the list of available fonts. Browse through the font options and click on the font you want to use. The selected text will automatically update to the new font.

2. Font size: Next to the font dropdown, you'll find the font size selector. You can manually input the font size or use the "+" and "-" buttons to increase or decrease the size.

BASIC TEXT EDITING

3. Changing Text Color: To change the color of the text, click on the "Color" drop-down menu in the text editing options. You can choose from predefined color palettes, or click on "rainbow color box with + icon" to access a color picker where you can select any color you desire.

4. Bold: Makes your text **Bold.**

5. Italic: Makes your text *italic.*

6. Alignments: The button next to Italic(I) is alignment. You can align your text left, right, center or justify it. Click on it and it will keep changing the alignment. Stop when you reach the right one.
Select Text Alignment:
- Left Alignment: The default alignment in Canva. Text is aligned to the left margin.
- Center Alignment: Text is centered horizontally on the canvas.
- Right Alignment: Text is aligned to the right margin.
- Justify Alignment: Text is aligned to both the left and right margins, creating even spacing between words in each line.

7. List: You can easily convert text to lists. There are 2 options bullet list and numbered list. Type your text each such that each text is on a separate line. Select all the text and click on the list Icon. It will toggle through bullet list and number list.

8. Letter and Line spacing: Adjust letter and Line spacing just by adjusting the slider to the point you want.

With Canva's user-friendly text editing tools, creating visually striking and professionally formatted text content becomes a simple and creative endeavor.

ADD, DELETE, DUPLICATE, LOCK, HIDE AND NAME PAGE

In Canva, you can easily manage your multi-page documents by adding, deleting, and duplicating pages.

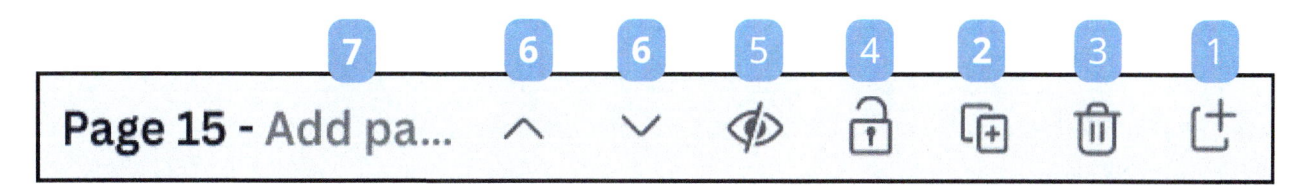

1. To Add a Page:
Just click on the + icon on top right of the page and it will add a new page. To add more pages repeat the same process.

2. To Duplicate a Page:
Just click on the Rectangle with + icon on top of the page and it will duplicate the page.

3. To Delete a Page:
Just click on the trashcan icon on top of the page and it will delete the page.

4. To Lock a page:
Just click on the Lock icon on top of the page and it will lock the page. To unlock it simply click on it again.

5. To Show/Hide a page:
Just click on the eye icon on top of the page and it will hide the page. To unhide or show it simply click on it again.

6. To move a page up or down:
Just click on the up arrow icon on top of the page and it will move the page up. Click on the down arrow icon on top of the page and it will move the page down.

7. To add page name:
Just click on the add a page title bar next to page number and type in the name you want.

With Canva's comprehensive page management features, users can effortlessly tailor their multi-page projects to achieve their desired design outcomes.

SHOW RULERS AND GUIDES

Rulers and guides in Canva are essential tools for precise design and layout. They help you align elements, maintain consistent spacing, and create professional-looking designs. Canva, being a user-friendly online design tool, also allows you to access rulers and guides to enhance your design precision.

To Show Rulers

To show Rulers and guides go to
File > View setting > show Rulers and guides
or simply press Shift+ R

To add guides

To show Rulers and guides go to
File > View setting > Add guides
You will get this pop up where we need to select guides
Here you get option to add 12, 6 or 3 column grid or you can also create custom grid.

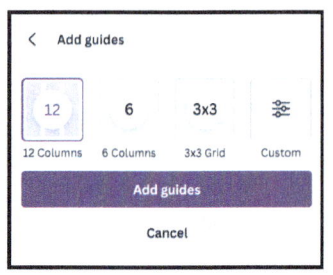

12 Column grid

6 Column grid

3 Column grid

Custom grid:
Just enter the number of columns and rows you want.
Enter gap and margin as well and click on Add guides

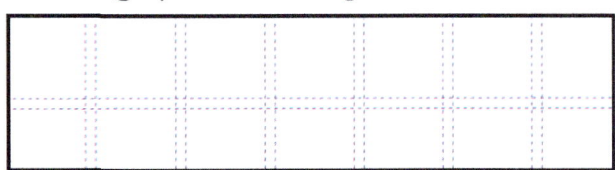

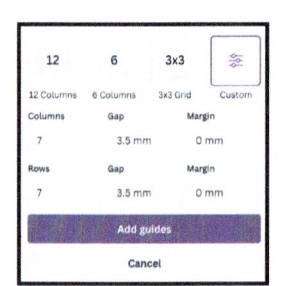

Using rulers and Guides can significantly enhance your design precision, allowing you to create visually appealing and well-structured projects with ease.

BLEEDS AND MARGINS

Bleeds and margins are critical elements in the design and printing process, ensuring that your printed materials appear as intended.

Bleeds extend the design beyond the page, preventing unwanted white borders.
margins create a safe zone for essential content.

Understanding how to set up bleeds and margins correctly is essential for professional print results.

To Show Margin

To show Margin go to
File > View setting > show Margin

To Hide Margin go to
File > View setting > show Margin

To Show Bleed

To show Rulers and guides go to
File > View setting > show Bleed

To Hide Margins and bleed go to
File > View setting > show Margin
all you have to do is just click on it again

This helps create print designs with precision. You can use margins to align elements and bleed to see all edges are printed properly.

TEXT EFFECTS

You can add effects such as drop shadows, outlines, and glows to your text to make it stand out.

Click on the "Effects" button on top bar of canvas

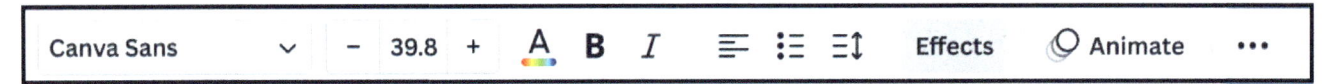

| Canva Sans | ∨ | − 39.8 + | A B I | ≡ ≔ ≡↕ | Effects | ◯ Animate | ⋯ |

Select "**shadow**" from the left bar of the screen.

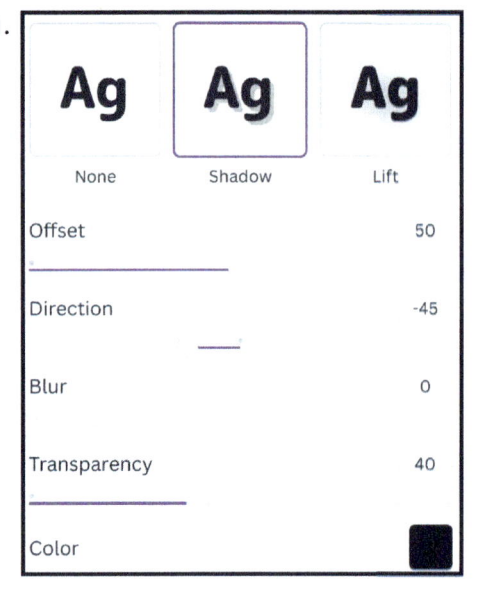

Adjust the settings such as
offset, Direction, blur, transparency and color.

Offset: Distance of shadow
Direction: sets the direction up, down,
            left or right.
Blur: set amount of blur
Transparency: sets the opacity of shadow.
Color: sets the color of shadow.

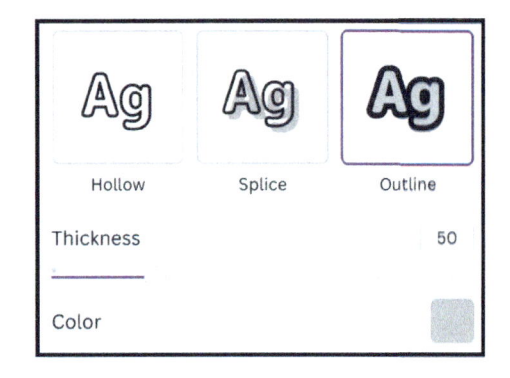

Outline:

Select "Outline" from the left bar of the screen.
Choose the outline color, thickness, and opacity.

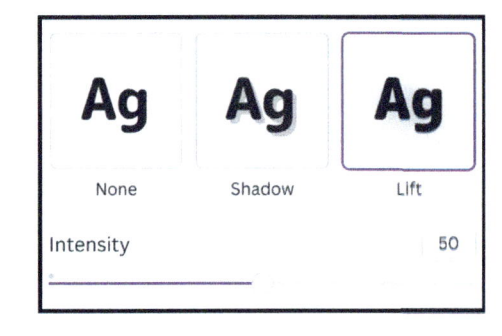

Lift Effect:

Choose "Lift" from the effects menu.
Adjust Intensity of color

21

TEXT EFFECTS

Hollow Effect:

Adjust thickness of the stroke.

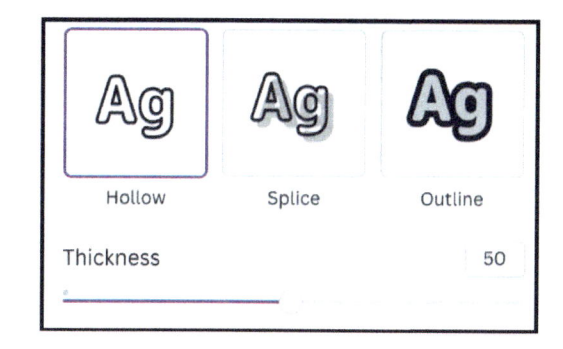

Echo

Adjust the settings for offset, direction and color

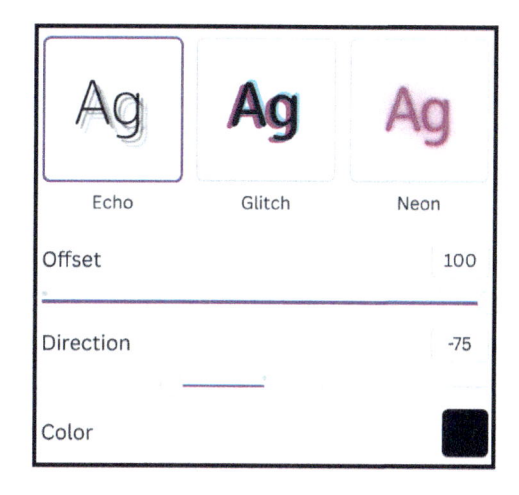

Neon Effect:

Adjust the Intensity of color

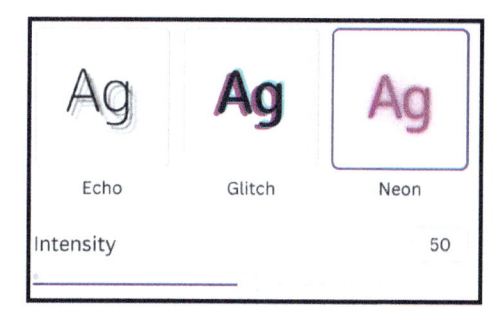

Background Effect:

This will add a background color to your text.

Adjust the roundness, spread, transparency and color of background

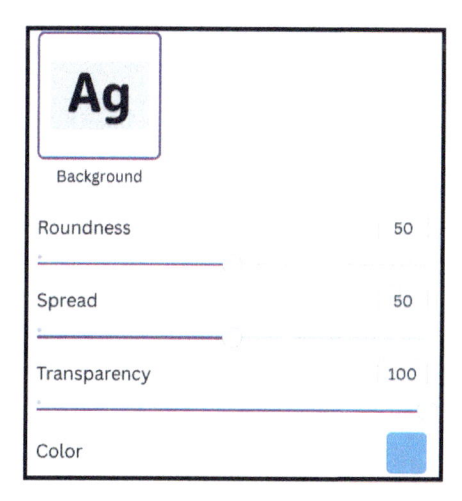

TEXT EFFECTS

Glitch Effect:

Adjust offset, direction and colors.

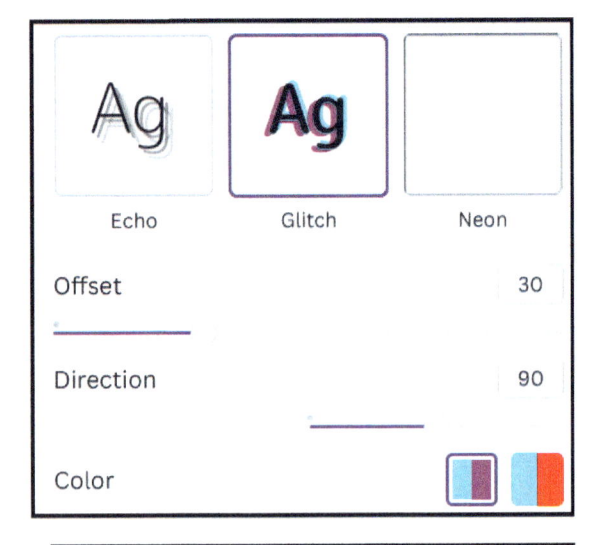

Splice Effect:

Adjust thickness, offset, direction and colors.

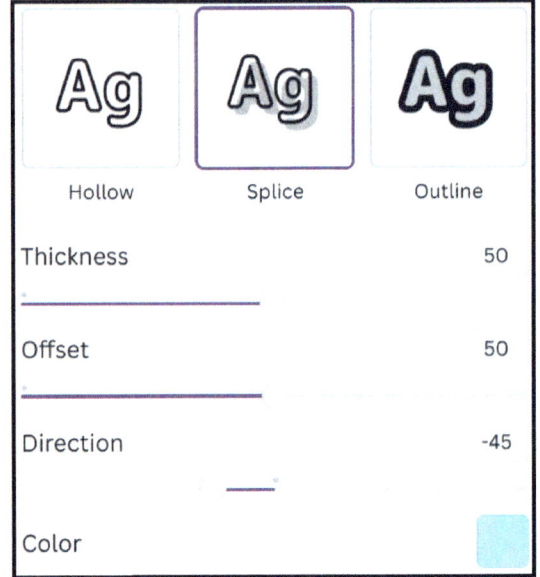

To remove the effect just click on None

Style

None   Shadow   Lift

ADDING DROP SHADOW

Canva offers a variety of effects and filters that can be used to enhance the visual appeal of your designs. In this chapter, we will explore the process of adding effects and filters to your designs.

Adding effects:

To add an drop shadow to your design, click on the image you want to apply the effect to. From the top bar select Edit Photo >

In the panel on the left side of the screen, click on the "Shadow" option.

Choose the type of effect you want to add, such as a drop shadow, glow or outline.

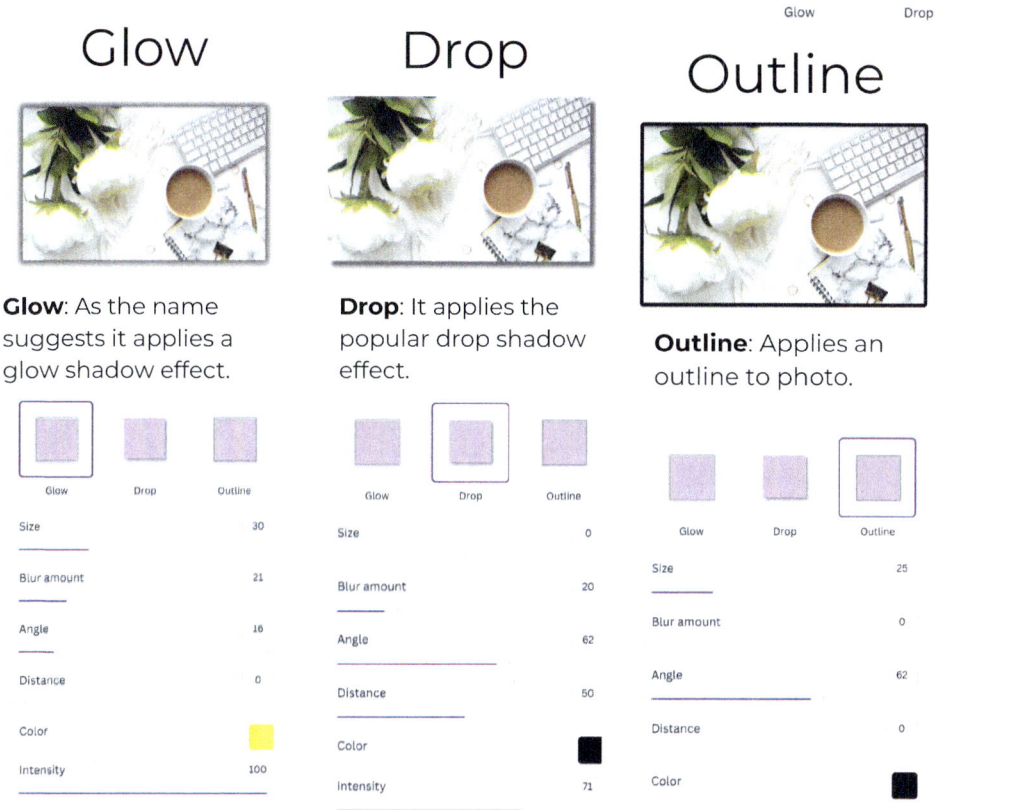

Glow

Glow: As the name suggests it applies a glow shadow effect.

- Size: 30
- Blur amount: 21
- Angle: 16
- Distance: 0
- Color: (yellow)
- Intensity: 100

Drop

Drop: It applies the popular drop shadow effect.

- Size: 0
- Blur amount: 20
- Angle: 62
- Distance: 50
- Color: (black)
- Intensity: 71

Outline

Outline: Applies an outline to photo.

- Size: 25
- Blur amount: 0
- Angle: 62
- Distance: 0
- Color: (black)
- Intensity: 100

You can customize the effect by adjusting its strength and more using the options in the panel.

Once you have added an effect to your element, you can further adjust it or remove it as needed.

ADDING COLOR

To give your design a cohesive and eye-catching look, you can experiment with backgrounds and colors.

Adding Background Color
Click on the background and select the color from the top bar

Adding Color to elements
Click on the element/shape and select the color from the top bar

Adding Color to text
Select the text and select the color from the top bar

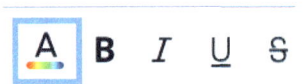

Color is a vital element in design, imbuing visual content with emotion, mood, and focus, making it an indispensable creative asset

GRADIENTS

After lots of request Canva finally has gradients. Now you can easily add gradients to background, frames and shapes.

How to add Gradient:

Select background, frame or shape. You'll see a bounding box around the image, indicating that it's selected.

Now click on the Color Icon on the Top bar.

Now click on the colorful Color Icon on the in the left bar, and click on Gradient

Click on the color icons and you can change the colors.

Then we have gradient style:
1. Linear: Applies Linear gradient from left to right
2. Vertical Linear: Applies Linear gradient from top to Bottom
3. Angular: Applies Angular gradient from top left to Bottom right
4. Radial: Applies radial gradient from outward to inward
5. Circular Angular: Applies radial gradient from outward to inward in angle from top left to Bottom right

How to add Gradient to frames:

Select frame You'll see a bounding box around the image, indicating that it's selected.

Apply a color.

Now click on the Color Icon on the Top bar.

Now click on the colorful Color Icon on the in the left bar, and click on Gradient

Gradients are a versatile design technique that seamlessly blends two or more colors, adding depth and dimension to visuals. They can evoke a sense of depth in designs.

ADD TEXT TO SHAPES

Adding text to shapes in Canva is a useful feature for creating customized labels, graphics, logos, and other visual elements. It allows you to integrate text seamlessly with shapes, enhancing your design creativity.

How to add text to shapes:
Go to elements tab and select the shape you want.
As soon as you click the image you will see a cursor inside the shape.
Simply start typing.
Now you can easily edit text just as we do,
Change font, size color, alignment from the top bar.

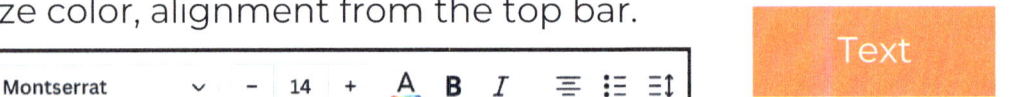

Change shape color from top bar as well

To change or edit text simply double click the shape.

You can add text to any shape.

SALE 50% OFF You can add text to any shape. SHOP NOW

Adding text to shapes in Canva empowers you to craft visually compelling designs, merging text and shapes harmoniously to convey your message effectively with ease.

FIND AND REPLACE

Discover the convenience of the 'Find and Replace' feature a time-saving tool that simplifies text editing in just a few clicks. This helps you find and replace text over entire document.

How to use:

Go to File > Select Find and Replace or simply press Clt +F

Find: Enter the text you want to find.
Replace with: Enter the text you want to replace the text with.
Check Match case if you want to match case ie. uppercase, lowercase.
Replace all: will replace all the text at once.
Replace: this will replace current text only.

The 'Find and Replace' tool in Canva streamlines text editing, saving you time and simplifying the process of refining your designs with precision.

COPY STYLE

In Canva, copying a style allows you to apply the same formatting, colors, and fonts from one element to another.

How to use copy style:

- Select the Source Element: Click on the element that has the style you want to copy. This will select the source element, and its style settings will be visible.

- Access the "Copy Style" Option:
  1. In the top toolbar, you'll find a "Copy Style" option an icon with a roller paint brush. or
  2. You will find this option right above the element selected. Click on the 3 dots and select Copy style or
  3. Simply press Clt + Alt + C

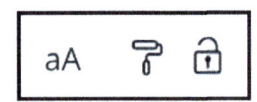

- Select the Target Element: After clicking "Copy Style," your cursor will turn into an filled paint roller icon.
  Click on the element you want to apply the copied style to. The target element's style will be updated to match the source element.

- Confirm the Style Copy: Review the target element to ensure the style has been copied and applied as desired.

Copying styles in Canva is a convenient way to maintain design consistency throughout your projects and save time when formatting elements with similar styles.

CONNECTING LINES AND SHAPES

In Canva, connecting lines and shapes can be a useful technique to create diagrams, flowcharts, and various design elements.

How to connect

- Add Shapes: Start by adding the shape you want to connect. Canva offers a variety of shapes and lines that you can use for your design. You can find them in the "Elements" panel on the left side of the canvas.

- Use Lines to Connect Shapes: Select a line element from the "Elements" panel and place it on the canvas.

- Now simply drag one end point of the line towards the shape and you will see it snap to shape. You can connect the line to any point of the shape that is highlighted with a white circle.

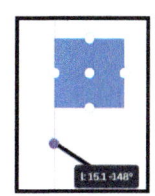

- once you connect line to shape it becomes one shape. now it will move together.

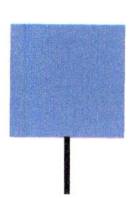

How to disconnect

To disconnect simply click and drag the point away from shape.

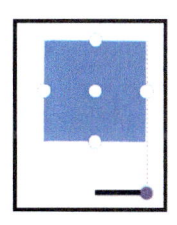

Connecting lines and shapes in Canva allows you to create visual representations, diagrams, and illustrations that effectively communicate ideas and information.

TEXT ON LINE

Adding text to a line in Canva is a creative way to convey information and create visually engaging designs.

How to add text to line

Add a Line: If you don't already have a line in your design, you can add one by selecting a line element from the "Elements" panel on the left side of the canvas. Simply click on the line and it will be added to the design.

Just double click on the line and you will see a text box on line.

Now simply type in your text

You can change font, font size, color of the text from the topbar.

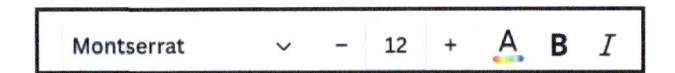

You can also move the text bar, when you place your cursor over the box you will see a hand icon. Then simply click and drag the box.

Change line style: Change the line style from the top bar, Click on the 3 line icon and select the line style you want. You can also change line weight.

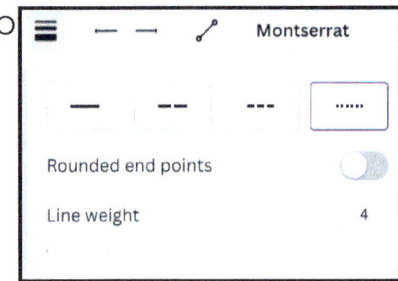

This is a easy way to create creative design with text and line in one stroke. You can also edit it easily.

FOLDERS

Folders in Canva help you maintain a tidy and organized workspace, making it easier to find and manage your designs, whether they're social media graphics, presentations, or any other creative projects. This feature is handy when you have a large number of designs and want to organize, categorize them for easy access.

Create a Folder:

From the home page go to left panel and click on Projects

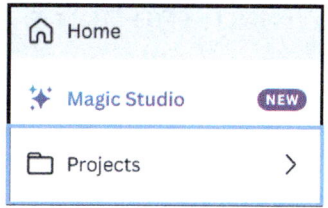

Here you will find all your files and designs. Click on the + Add new button on the top right and select Folder

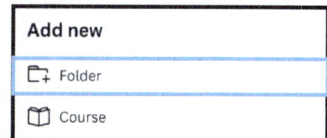

Add folder name and click on Continue

Delete Folder:
From the home page go to left panel and click on Projects.

Click on folders

Click on Check the box on the left top of the folder and click the Delete icon (trash can icon) on the bottom

Canva's folder feature simplifies design organization, offering a streamlined way to manage and access your creations. Keep your creative workspace in order and enhance your productivity.

ACCESS DESIGNS

Canva's user-friendly interface makes it simple to access your designs, You can easily find, open and edit any design you created in Canva.

There are many ways you can access your designs.
1. From Homepage: When you open Canva on the home page itself you will see your recent designs. just click on the design you want and it will open. now you can edit it.
2. From the home page fo the left bar of the screen and click on projects.

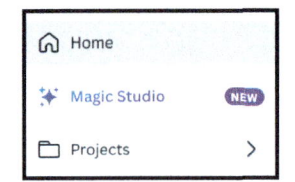

here you will find all your designs. Just click on the design you want and it will open

> Canva's user-friendly interface ensures that your designs are easily accessible, whether you're picking up where you left off, sharing your work, or downloading your creations.

DUPLICATE DESIGN

One useful feature in Canva is the "Duplicate" function, which allows users to replicate their designs with ease. Duplicating a design in Canva can be a time-saving and efficient way to create multiple versions of the same design or work on a project with similar elements.

How to duplicate your design:

There are several ways to do this,

1. Open file: Open the file you want to duplicate, then go to File> Make a copy

2. From Home Page go the left side panel of the screen and select Projects, on the right side you will see all your designs, Click on the 3 dots on top right of the design thumbnail and select Make a copy

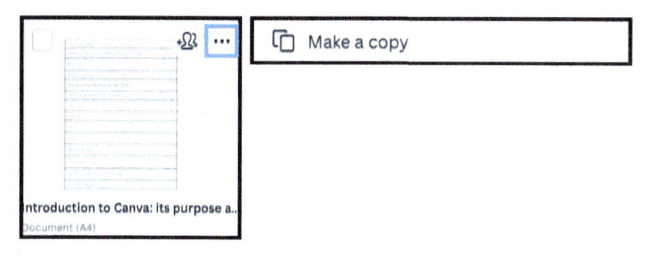

Duplicating designs helps create multiple versions of the design without recreating it from scratch and experiment with different designs.

34

TABLES

Tables are a versatile and commonly used tool for organizing and presenting data in a structured and easily understandable format. They are widely employed in various fields, including business, education, research, and web design. In a table, information is organized into rows and columns, creating a grid-like structure that facilitates data comparison and reference.

How to Add table

- Access the Elements Panel: On the left-hand side of your Canva workspace, you'll find the "Elements" panel. Click on it.
- Search for "Table": In the Elements panel, scroll down to the Table section and click See all
- Add the Table: Click on the table element you want to use onto your design canvas.

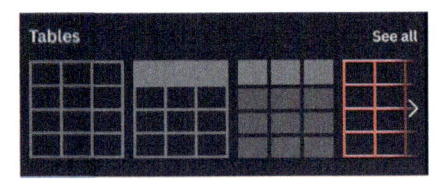

Editing Table

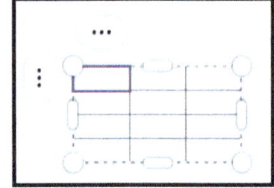

- Adding Rows and Columns: Click on any cell and you will see 3 dots icon on top and side as well. Click on it and you will get options to edit.
- If you click on the Top 3 Dots you will options to Edit Columns and If you click on the sides 3 dots you will get options to edit rows.
- When you click on the Top 3 Dots you will options to Add and Delete Column. You can also move the column left or right simply by clicking on Move Column to left or move Column to Right option 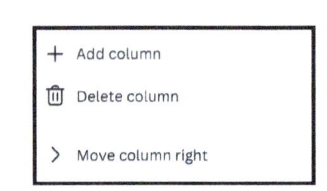
- When you click on the Side 3 Dots you will get options to Add and Delete row. You can also move the row up or down simply by clicking on Move row to up or move row to down option 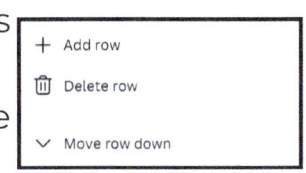
- To add fill color to cell click on the cell and select a fill color from top bar.

TABLES

Editing Table

- Adding Text and Data: Click within a cell to add text or data.
- Styling and Formatting: To style the table, you can use the formatting options in the top bar, such as changing the font, font size, text color, and cell background color.
- Merging Cells: You can merge cells to create larger cells for headers or more complex layouts. Select the cells you want to merge, click on the 3 dots next to table and choose "Merge cells."
- Borders and Lines: Canva allows you to add or remove borders for cells and the table. You can adjust border colors and styles to match your design.
Click on the grid icon on the top bar and select border style by clicking on the 3 line icon

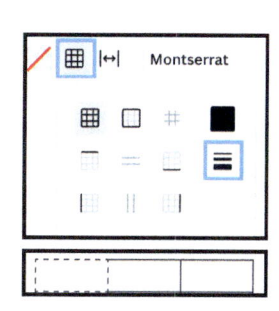

- Resizing Columns and Rows: Click and drag the column or row borders to adjust their sizes as needed.

- Sizing column equally: To size all columns equally, Click on the top 3 dots icon above the table and select size column equally.
- Sizing row equally: To size all rows equally, Click on the side 3 dots icon next to the table and select size row equally.
- Sizing row and column to content: To size all rows and column to content, Click on the side 3 dots icon next to the table and select size row to content or size column to content.

- Deleting the Table: To delete the entire table, click on it to select it, and then press the Delete or Backspace key on your keyboard.

Incorporate tables into your designs to maintain data clarity and enhance visual appeal. From basic data organization to more advanced designs, table provide users options for visualizing and structuring information.

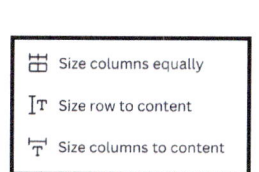

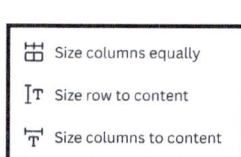

INTRODUCTION TO FRAMES

Frames and grids are two essential tools in Canva that help you create well-structured designs. In this chapter, you will learn how to use frames and grids in Canva and how they can be used to improve the overall design of your projects.

Frames

Frames are used to define the boundaries of your design and ensure that all elements are contained within the designated area. In Simple words frames are containers for your photos.

To select a frame got to elements tab then scroll down until you find Frames section. then click see all.

Then simply click on the frame you want and it will be placed on the canvas.

Then simply drag the photo in the frame

And there you have it. Your Photo in frame!

There are many frames with various shapes. You can browse through all of them and select a frame that suits your design.

INTRODUCTION TO GRIDS

Grids are used to align elements in your design and provide a visual structure. They help you create balance and symmetry in your designs and ensure that elements are aligned and spaced evenly. In Canva, you can choose from a range of pre-made grids or create your own custom grid.

Grids

To select a frame go to elements tab then scroll down until you find Grid section.

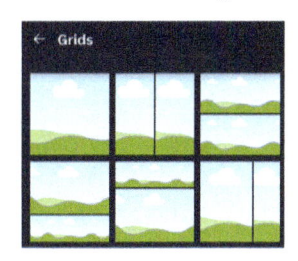

Then click see all.

Then select the type of grid you want to use.

Just click on the grid you want and it will be added to the canvas.

Then simply drag the photo in the grids.

There you have it all photos in the gird

There are many grids with various shapes. You can browse through all of them and select a grid that suits your design.

38

INTRODUCTION TO GRIDS

You can adjust the size of the grid spacing between them to fit your design needs. Select spacing from top bar.

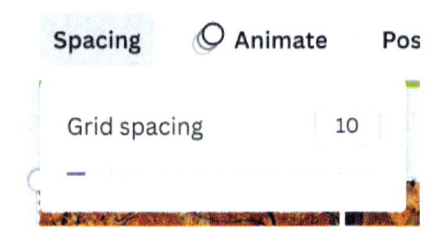

It's important to keep in mind that while frames and grids provide a structure for your design, they should not be used to limit your creativity. You can still add elements outside of the frame and grid, or adjust the size and position of elements to create a unique and creative design.

Tips for Using Frames and Grids in Canva

Here are some tips to help you get the most out of frames and grids in Canva:

- Experiment with different frame sizes to see what works best for your design.
- Use the grid to align elements, but don't be afraid to break away from it if necessary.
- Adjust the spacing of the grid cells to fit your design needs.
- Use the frame to define the boundaries of your design, but don't be afraid to extend elements outside of it for creative effect.

There are many grids with various shapes. You can browse through all of them and select a grid that suits your design.

STAR A TEMPLATE, PHOTO AND ELEMENTS

Staring a template, photo and elements makes it easy for you to find it easily later. Canva has millions of template, photo and elements, so scrolling through you may come across something you like. Once you star it you can easily find it later.

How to star a template:

When browsing templates from design tab in the left of the screen. Click on the 3 dots on the top right of the template. It will display all the information about it. Down you will find a Star icon. Just click on it.

How to star a element:

When browsing elements from element tab in the left of the screen. Click on the 3 dots on the top right of the element.
It will display all the information about it.
Down you will find a Star icon. Just click on it.

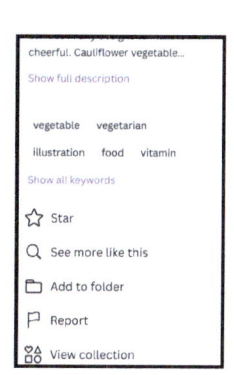

How to star a Photo:

When browsing photo from design tab in the left of the screen. Click on the 3 dots on the top right of the element.
It will display all the information about it.
Down you will find a Star icon. Just click on it.

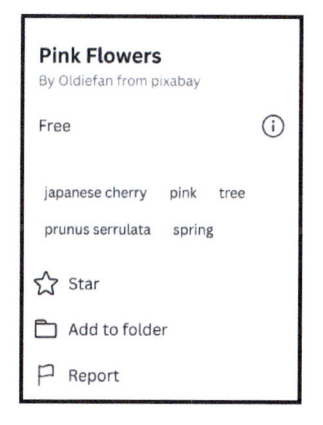

How to unstar

Just click on the 3 dots again and click on the star again.

This is a easy way to find templates, photo and elements. This simplifies design process as you have all the things you need in one place.

40

CHOOSING TEMPLATES AND CUSTOMIZING DESIGNS

Canva offers a wide range of templates that can be used as a starting point for your designs. In this chapter, we will explore the process of choosing a template and customizing it to fit your needs.

Choosing a template

1. To access Canva's templates, click on the "Templates" tab from the left side of the screen

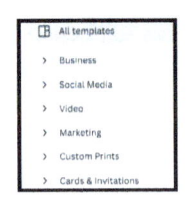

You will see a list of templates organized by category, such as social media graphics, presentations, invitations, and more.

2. When you click on any of the options will get a whole list of templates for that category.

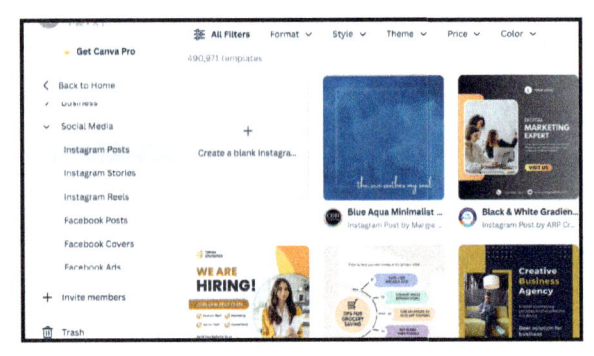

3. Browse through the templates and choose one that best fits your design needs.

4. Once you select the template you want, Click on it and you will get a pop window, in that pop up window click Customize this template and you are ready to customize the template as per your requirements.

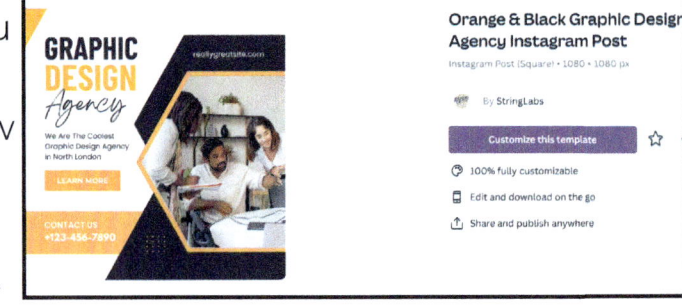

41

EXPORTING AND SHARING DESIGNS

Once you have completed your design in Canva, you can easily export and share it with others. In this chapter, we will explore the process of exporting and sharing designs using Canva.

Exporting designs:

To export a design, click on the "Share" button in the top right corner of the screen. Then select download.

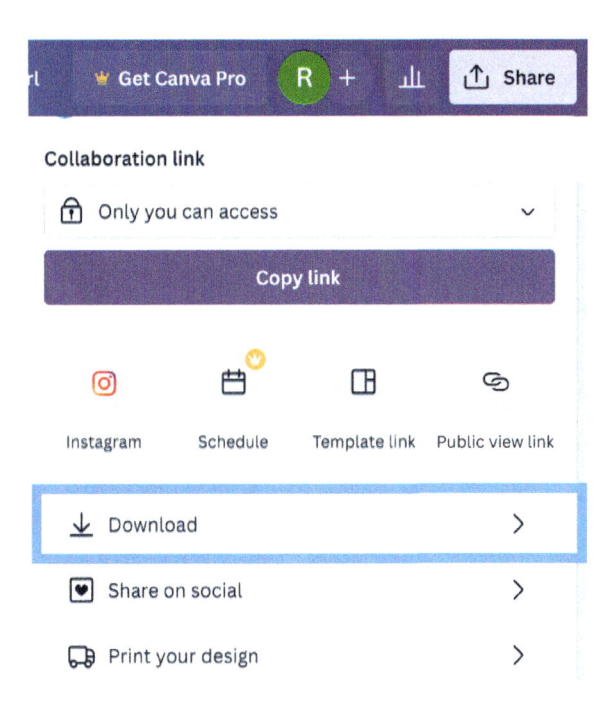

Choose the file format you want to export the design as, such as JPG, PNG, or PDF.

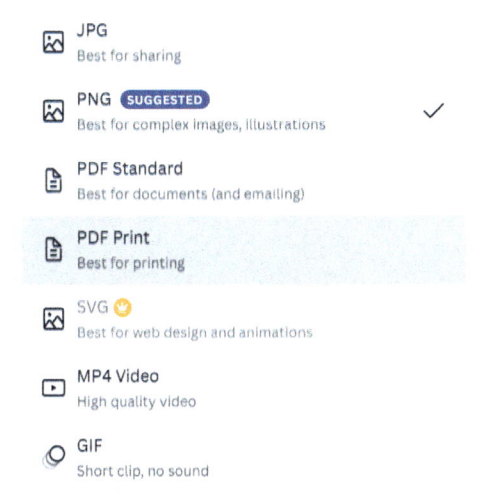

42

EXPORTING AND SHARING DESIGNS

You can also choose the quality and size of the exported file.

```
Size ×                                          1
─────────○──────────────────
1,080 × 1,080 px                                👑

Quality                                         80
──────────────────────○─────
File size: Large                                👑
```

Once you have made your selections, click on the "Download" button to download the file to your computer.

Sharing designs on Social media:

To share a design, click on the "Share" button in the top right corner of the screen. Then click on Share on social. You can directly publish designs from Canva to your socials.

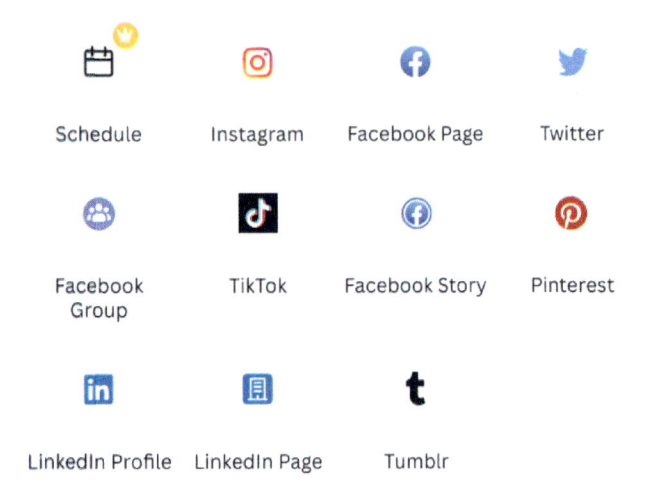

Schedule   Instagram   Facebook Page   Twitter

Facebook Group   TikTok   Facebook Story   Pinterest

LinkedIn Profile   LinkedIn Page   Tumblr

Just Click on the social media icon you want. Connect your account and you are good to go.

> In conclusion, Canva makes it easy to export and share designs with others. It provides a variety of options for exporting and sharing designs with others. With its user-friendly interface and variety of file formats, Canva is the ideal tool for exporting and sharing your designs with others.

COLLABORATING WITH OTHERS ON DESIGNS

Canva makes it easy to collaborate with others on designs, regardless of where you are located or what time it is. In this chapter, we will explore the process of collaborating with others on designs using Canva. One of the most powerful features of Canva is its ability to facilitate collaboration and seamless sharing of your designs. Whether you're working on a team project, seeking feedback, or sharing your creations with the world, Canva offers a range of tools to help you collaborate effectively and distribute your designs efficiently. In this chapter, we'll explore how to collaborate, share, and manage your designs using Canva's collaborative features.

Inviting Collaborators

Collaboration in Canva allows multiple users to work on a single design together: Open your design and click on the "Share" button in the top right corner.

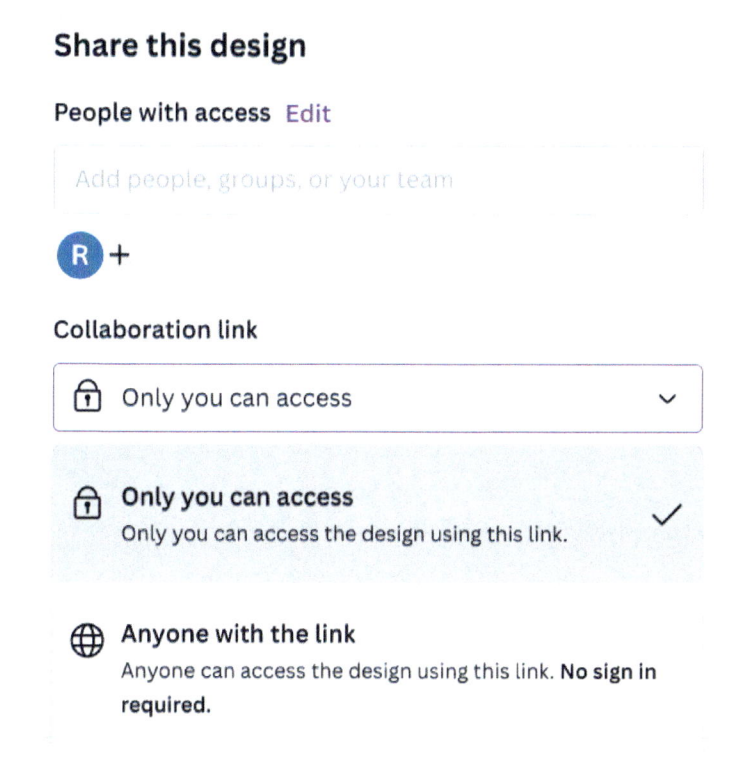

Share this design

People with access Edit

[Add people, groups, or your team]

(R) +

Collaboration link

[🔒 Only you can access ▼]

🔒 **Only you can access** ✓
Only you can access the design using this link.

🌐 **Anyone with the link**
Anyone can access the design using this link. **No sign in required.**

Invite Collaborators: Enter the email addresses of the collaborators you want to invite in the People with access field.

Assign Roles: Choose the role for each collaborator—
Can comment, edit or View.

COLLABORATING WITH OTHERS ON DESIGNS

Collaboration Link: Here you can set permission as to who can access the design with this link. You can choose to Keep the design access to yourself or can share it with anyone with this link.

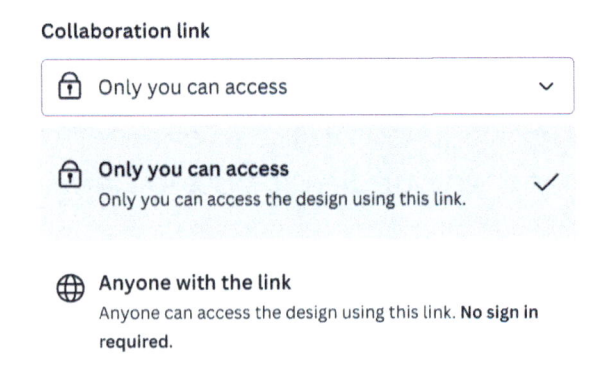

Collaboration link

| 🔒 Only you can access | ⌄ |

🔒 **Only you can access** ✓
Only you can access the design using this link.

🌐 **Anyone with the link**
Anyone can access the design using this link. **No sign in required.**

Work simultaneously with others on the same design

Editing Simultaneously: When collaborators are in the design, you can see their cursor, changes, and selections in real time.
Chat and Comments: Communicate with collaborators using the chat and comment features to discuss changes and suggestions.

Working on designs together:

When multiple people are working on the same design, each person's changes will be reflected in real-time.

You can communicate with others by leaving comments.

Canva also has a version history feature, which allows you to view previous versions of the design and revert to a previous version if necessary.
This is pro feature only.

> In conclusion, Canva's collaboration features make it easy to work with others on designs, regardless of location or time. The platform's real-time updates, chat function, and version history feature ensure that everyone is on the same page and that the design process is as seamless as possible. Whether you are working with a team of designers, a client, or just a friend, Canva is the ideal tool for collaborating on designs.

UNDERSTANDING FILE TYPES

In this chapter, we will cover the different file types available in Canva and when to use each one. By understanding the different file types, you can choose the right format to suit your needs and ensure that your designs look great no matter where they are used.

PNG (Portable Network Graphics)
PNG is a lossless image format that is commonly used for web graphics. It is ideal for designs that have a transparent background, such as logos, icons, and graphics with text or illustrations. PNG files support transparency, which means you can place them over any color or pattern without having a solid white background.

JPG (Joint Photographic Experts Group)
JPG is a popular image format that is used for photographs and other images with complex color and detail. Unlike PNG, JPG does not support transparency, but it provides a high level of compression and smaller file sizes, making it ideal for sharing and uploading online.

PDF (Portable Document Format)
PDF is a universal file format that is ideal for sharing and printing. It is commonly used for invoices, flyers, and other designs that need to be printed or sent as a document. PDF files are also great for sharing presentations or portfolios because they preserve the original design and formatting, regardless of the device or software being used to view them.

UNDERSTANDING FILE TYPES

GIF (Graphic Interchange Format)
GIF is a lossless image format that is commonly used for short animations and animated logos. It is also ideal for designs that need to be small in file size and easy to share online. The downside of GIF is that it only supports 256 colors, so it may not be suitable for high-quality designs with lots of detail.

GIF

MP4 (MPEG-4 Part 14)
MP4 is a video file format that is commonly used for sharing and uploading videos online. It is ideal for short animations and video presentations. MP4 files can be easily embedded on websites and social media platforms, making it easy to share your designs with a wider audience.

In conclusion, by understanding the different file types available in Canva, you can choose the right format to suit your needs and ensure that your designs look great no matter where they are used. Whether you're creating a logo, flyer, presentation, or video, Canva has the tools you need to bring your designs to life.

APPLYING EFFECTS TO PHOTO

Applying effects to photos in Canva is a great way to enhance and stylize your images for your designs. There are tons of effects that you can apply.

Applying Filters to photo
1. Add a Photo:
    - If you're not working with a photo already in your design, you can add one by clicking on the "Elements" tab in the left sidebar and then selecting "Photos." Choose the photo you want to edit, and it will be added to your canvas.
2. Select the Photo:
    - Click on the photo in your canvas to select it. You'll know it's selected when you see a bounding box and editing options.
3. Access the "Effects" Menu:
    - In the top toolbar, you should see an "Edit Photo"

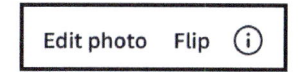

   Click on it to open then find the Filter section and click on See all. You'll have a variety of effects to choose from.

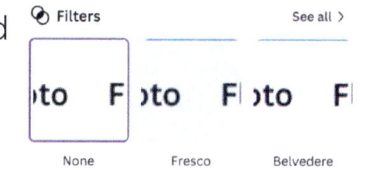

Filter Effects:
   - In the "Filter" section, you can apply various filters to your photo. These filters can change the color, mood, and style of the photo. Click on a filter to apply it, and you can adjust the intensity using the slider that appears

Now lets apply Filters to this photo

APPLYING EFFECTS TO PHOTO

Natural filters

Fresco  Myst  Flint  Luna

In each of these you just have to adjust the intensity.

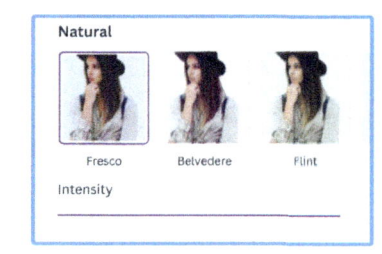

Warm filters

Latte  Bronz  Sandi  Sangri

In each of these you just have to adjust the intensity.

APPLYING EFFECTS TO PHOTO

Cool filters

Scandi    Arctic    Polar    Tundra

In each of these you just have to adjust the intensity.

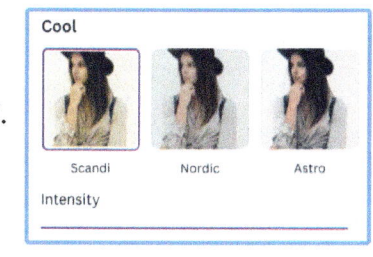

Vivid filters

Vivid    Eldar    Aria    Stark

In each of these you just have to adjust the intensity.

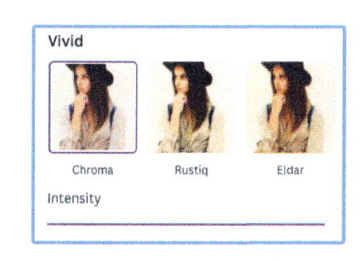

APPLYING EFFECTS TO PHOTO

Soft filters

Aura    Whimsi    Oceanic    Nimbus

In each of these you just have to adjust the intensity.

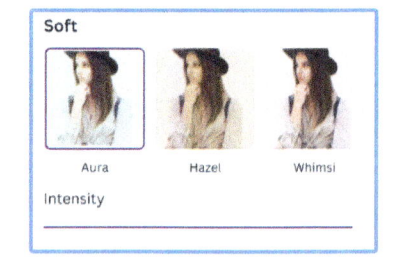

Vintage filters

Vinto    Antiq    Dream    Retro

In each of these you just have to adjust the intensity.

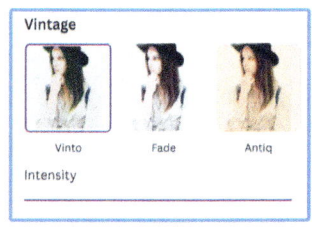

APPLYING EFFECTS TO PHOTO

Mono filters

Classic  | Ink  | Film  | Newspaper

In each of these you just have to adjust the intensity.

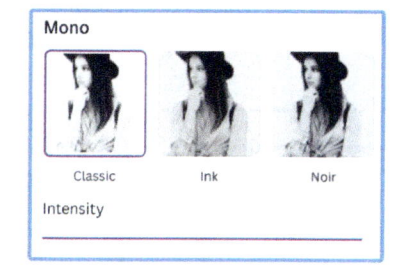

Color Pop filters

outrun  | Heatwave  | Amethyst  | X Pro +

In each of these you just have to adjust the intensity.

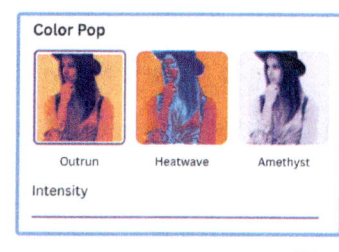

ADDING OUTLINE TO PHOTOS

In Canva, adding an outline or border to photos or elements is a great way to make them stand out or add a decorative touch to your designs.

Select the Photo: Click on the photo you want to outline to select it. You'll see a bounding box around the image, indicating that it's selected.

Now click on the Border Icon on the Topbar.

Set the border size and style. There are 4 line styles to choose from.

Corner Rounding: You can also add rounded corners just by setting this value.

Color: You can change border color by clicking on the color icon next to border icon. Set the color you want.

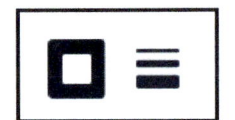

> Adding an outline to photos in Canva is an effective way to make your images more visually engaging and create a unique design style. It's especially useful when you want to make specific elements in your design stand out or match your branding.

53

CROP PHOTO

Cropping a photo in Canva is a simple process and can help you focus on a specific part of the image or adjust its dimensions to fit your design.

- Select the Photo:
    - Click on the photo you want to crop to select it. You'll see a bounding box around the image, indicating that it's selected.

- Access the "Crop" Tool:
    - In the top toolbar, you'll find a "Edit Photo" option. Click on Crop.

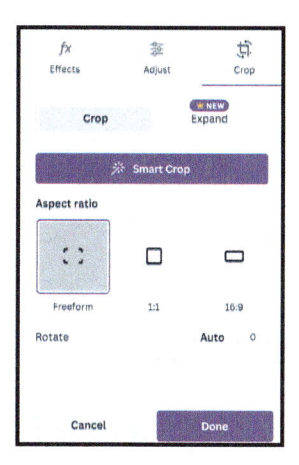

- Adjust the Crop:
    - You can crop the photo freeform or in many aspect ratios.

- Move the Crop Area:
    - If you need to reposition the area you want to crop, click inside the photo and drag it to the desired position within the crop frame.

54

CROP PHOTO

- Rotate: You can also rotate your photo if you want to. just move the slider to adjust it. you can also click on Auto to automatically adjust the rotate.

- Apply the Crop: Once you're satisfied with the cropping, click the "Done" button to confirm the crop. Your photo will be cropped according to your adjustments.

Method 2

Simply double click on the photo, you will enter the crop mode. Now drag the corner handle to the point you wan to crop.

When in the crop mode click on the image to move and adjust the photo position and scale. To scale the photo drag the bound box of photo.

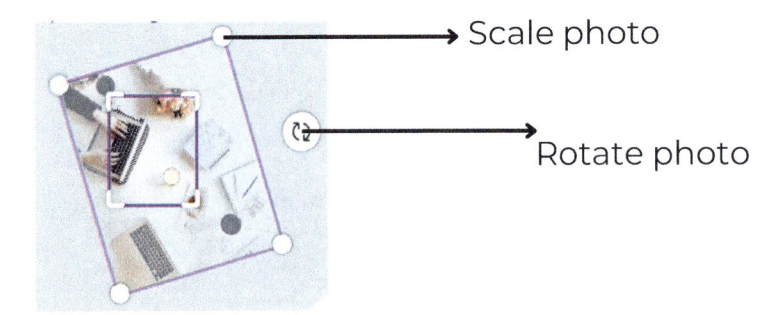

Scale photo

Rotate photo

To rotate the image click and drag the rotate icon.

FLIP PHOTO

Flipping a photo in Canva is a useful technique to flip the image horizontally or vertically. Many time you need to do this in order to match your design. It can also be use to create mirrored or inverted versions of an image.

- Select the Photo:
  Click on the photo you want to flip to select it. You'll see a bounding box around the image, indicating that it's selected.

- Access the "Flip" Tool:
  In the top toolbar, you'll find a "Flip" option with horizontal and vertical arrows.

Click on either the horizontal or vertical flip icon to mirror the photo accordingly.

    Horizontal Flip: This flips the photo horizontally from left to right.

    Vertical Flip: This flips the photo vertically from top to bottom.

TRANSPARENCY

Transparency or opacity can be easily adjusted in Canva. This can be useful to create many effects

1. Select the Element:
   - Click on the element you wish to make transparent to select it. You'll see a bounding box around the element, indicating that it's selected.
2. Access the "Transparency" Tool:
   - In the top toolbar, you'll find a "Transparency" option. Click on it to open the transparency tool.
3. Adjust the Transparency:
   - When you activate the "Transparency" tool, you'll typically see a slider that allows you to adjust the transparency of the selected element.
   - Moving the slider to the left will decrease the transparency, making the element more opaque.
   - Moving it to the right will increase the transparency, making the element more see-through.

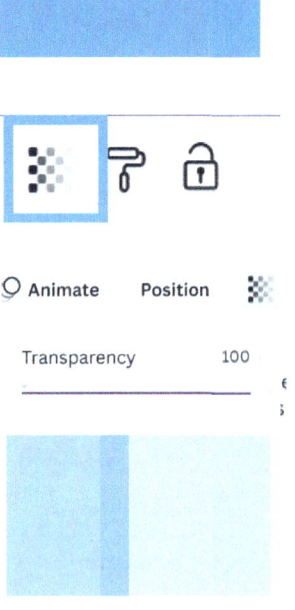

Adjusting transparency is useful when you want to overlay elements, create subtle backgrounds, or emphasize certain parts of your design. It can add depth and sophistication to your visuals and allow elements to interact more harmoniously within your composition. Canva's transparency tool offers flexibility in fine-tuning your designs.

LOCK

Locking elements in Canva is a useful feature that allows you to prevent accidental movement or changes to specific elements in your design. This can be particularly handy when you want to maintain the positioning and styling of certain elements while continuing to work on other parts of your design.

- Select the Element:
    - Click on the element you wish to lock to select it. You'll see a bounding box around the element, indicating that it's selected.
- Access the "Lock" Tool:
    - In the top toolbar, you'll find a "Lock" option.
    - Click on it to lock the selected element.
- Confirm Locking:
  After clicking the "Lock" option, the selected element will be locked. You'll typically see a padlock icon on the element to indicate that it's now locked.
- Prevent Movement and Edits:
  Locked elements cannot be moved, resized, or edited until they are unlocked. This helps maintain their position and styling as you continue to work on other elements of your design.
- Unlocking Elements:
  If you want to make changes to a locked element, select it, and click the "Unlock" option in the top toolbar. This will remove the padlock icon, and you can then edit the element as needed.
- Locking Multiple Elements:
  You can also lock multiple elements simultaneously by selecting multiple elements and then clicking the "Lock" option. This is useful for maintaining the alignment and arrangement of grouped elements.

Locking elements in Canva is a valuable tool for maintaining control and consistency in your designs. It ensures that specific elements stay in place, allowing you to work on your design with confidence without worrying about unintended changes.

GROUPING

Grouping elements in Canva is a helpful feature that allows you to select and manipulate multiple elements together as a single unit. This can be particularly useful when you want to maintain the relative positioning and arrangement of elements in your design.

- Select Multiple Elements: Click on the first element you want to include in the group to select it. You'll see a bounding box around the selected element. To select multiple elements, hold down the "Shift" key on your keyboard while clicking on each element you want to include in the group.

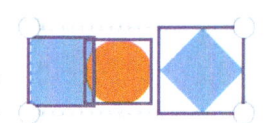

- Access the "Group" Option: When you select multiple elements, you'll find a "Group" option right above the elements selected. Click on it to group the selected elements. Or right click and select group.

- Confirm Grouping: After clicking the "Group" option, the selected elements will be grouped together. You'll typically see a bounding box around the entire group, indicating that they are now part of a single unit.

- Manipulate the Group: Once elements are grouped, you can move, resize, and rotate the entire group as one unit. Any changes you make to one element within the group will affect the entire group.

- Ungrouping Elements: If you want to ungroup elements, select the grouped elements, and click the "Ungroup" option in the top toolbar. This will separate the elements, allowing you to edit them individually.

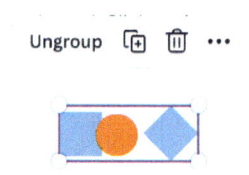

Grouping elements is a practical way to keep related design elements together and maintain their relative positions as you work on your design. It simplifies the editing process, especially when you need to apply consistent adjustments to multiple elements at once.

DELETING

Deleting elements in Canva is a straightforward process and allows you to remove unwanted objects or design components from your project.

Select the Element to Delete: Click on the element you want to delete to select it. You'll see a bounding box around the selected element, indicating that it's chosen.

Delete the Element: Once the element is selected, you can delete it in one of the following ways:
- Press the "Delete" or "Backspace" key on your keyboard.
- Right-click on the selected element and choose "Delete" from the context menu.
- Use the "Delete" option the appear just on top of the element that you select.

> Deleting is as simple as just clicking the Delete key on your keyboard. Delete unwanted elements with ease.

DUPLICATE ELEMENTS

Duplicating elements in Canva is a convenient way to create copies of objects, making it easy to maintain consistency or reuse specific design elements.

- Select the Element to Duplicate:
  Click on the element you want to duplicate to select it. You'll see a bounding box around the selected element, indicating that it's chosen.
- Duplicate the Element:
  Once the element is selected, you can duplicate it in one of the following ways:
    - Press the "Ctrl" key (Windows) or "Command" key (Mac) on your keyboard and then press the "D" key.
    - Right-click on the selected element and choose "Duplicate" from the context menu.
    - Use the "Duplicate" option that appears right on top of the element selected, which often appears as two overlapping squares or rectangles with a + sign.
- Confirmation:
  Canva will create a duplicate of the selected element and place it next to the original.
- Reposition or Edit the Duplicate:
  The duplicated element will typically appear on top of the original. You can now reposition, resize, or edit the duplicate as needed.
- Additional Duplicates:
  If you need multiple duplicates of the same element, simply repeat the process by selecting the element and duplicating it again.

Quick tips: To make more copies just duplicate it once and then simply press clt + D and it will keep making copies

> Duplicating elements is a time-saving feature that simplifies the design process, especially when you need to maintain consistency across your project or reuse certain design components.

POSITION: ARRANGING ELEMENTS

Canva provides a range of arrangement tools to help you precisely position and arrange elements in your designs.

- Select the Elements to Align: Click on the first element you want to align to select it. Hold down the "Shift" key (Windows) or "Command" key (Mac) and click on additional elements to select multiple elements.
- Access the "arrange" Options: In the top toolbar, you'll typically find Position option. Click on it to access the arrange settings on the left side of the screen.

- **Change Layering Order:** Within the "Arrange" settings, you can,
1. Bring the element forward or backward in relation to other elements.
2. Move the element to the front or back of all elements on the canvas.
3. Place the element at the top or bottom of the layering order.

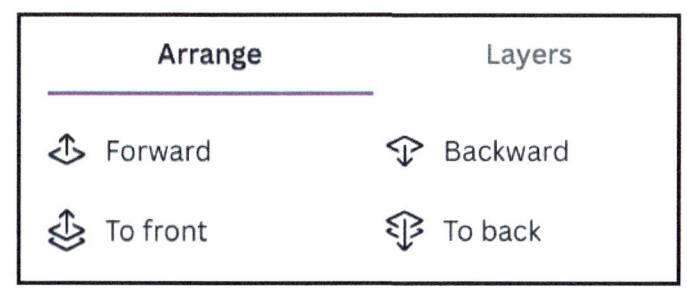

Arrange	Layers
Forward	Backward
To front	To back

- In short forward will bring the element 1 step up and backward will take it down one step.
- To front will bring the element to the top of all elements while To back will take it to the back of all elements

| See the top light orange box | Backward | To Back | See the back light orange box now lets bring it forward | Forward | To Front |

Positioning and arranging elements in Canva allows you to fine-tune the layout and layering of design components. Whether you're aligning text and graphics for a polished look or adjusting the layering order to control which elements appear in front of others, these tools provide you with precise control over your designs.

POSITION: ALIGNING ELEMENTS

Canva provides a range of alignment tools to help you precisely position and align elements in your designs.

- Select the Elements to Align: Click on the first element you want to align to select it. Hold down the "Shift" key (Windows) or "Command" key (Mac) and click on additional elements to select multiple elements.
- Access the "Alignment" Options: In the top toolbar, you'll typically find Position option. Click on it to access the alignment settings on the left side of the screen.

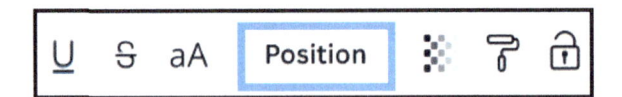

- Choose the Alignment Type: From the alignment menu, select the type of alignment you want to apply. For example, you can choose "Center" to center elements vertically.
  When you select only one element or a group you can align it to the page.

When you select multiple elements you can align it to the elements

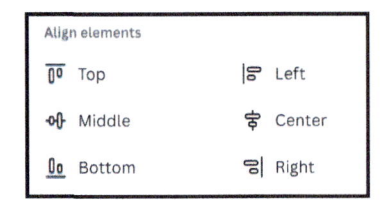

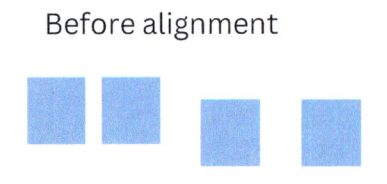

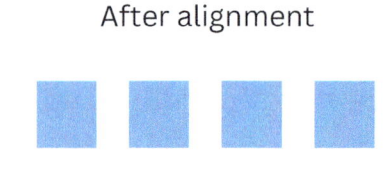

- Distribute Horizontally:
  Evenly spaces selected elements horizontally between the first and last elements.
- Distribute Vertically:
  Evenly spaces selected elements vertically between the first and last elements.

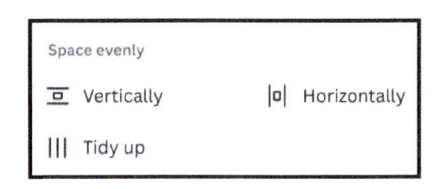

By utilizing Canva's alignment tools, you can easily achieve pixel-perfect layouts and ensure that elements in your designs are perfectly aligned, evenly spaced, and visually pleasing.

POSITION: ALIGNING ELEMENTS

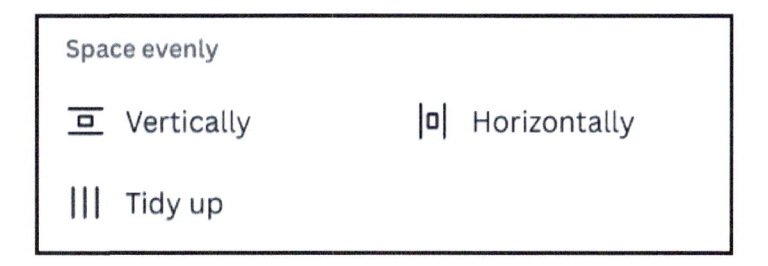

```
Space evenly

 ▭  Vertically        |▫|  Horizontally

 |||  Tidy up
```

Distribute Horizontally: Evenly spaces selected elements horizontally between the first and last elements.

Distribute Vertically: Evenly spaces selected elements vertically between the first and last elements.

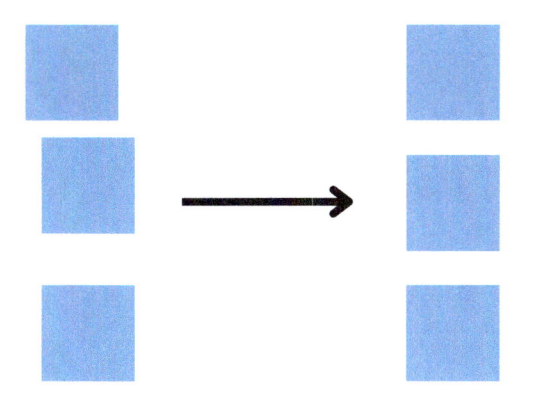

Tidy Up: This will align and evenly space elements.

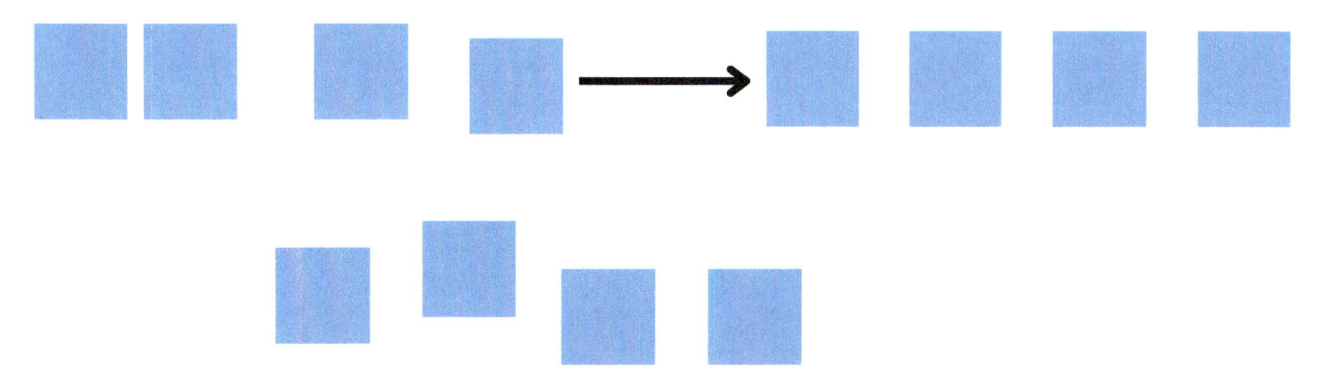

> These additional alignment and distribution options in Canva allow you to achieve even more control over the layout of your designs.

POSITION: PLACING ELEMENTS AND SETTING DIMENSIONS

- Select the Element to Position: Click on the element you want to position to select it. You'll see a bounding box around the selected element, indicating that it's chosen.
- Access the "Position" Options: In the top toolbar, you'll typically find a "Position" option.

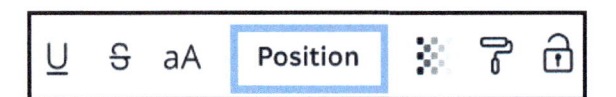

Click on it to access the position settings on the left side of the screen.

- Adjust Position: Within the "Position" settings, you can Change the element's X and Y coordinates to move it horizontally and vertically.

- Set the element's width and height. You can also lock ratio of width to height by clicking on the lock icon.
- Alter the element's rotation angle by entering the angle of rotation.

> By adjusting the width, height, and rotation of elements in Canva, you can achieve precise control over the layout and orientation of your design, creating visually engaging and customized compositions.

LAYERS

Layers panel is the latest addition to Canva arsenal. This was the much awaited feature and now it is finally here. Layers help you access your elements with ease.

Accessing Layers Panel:
Select a element, then in the Top-bar you will see Position button. Click on it to access layers panel on the left side of the screen.

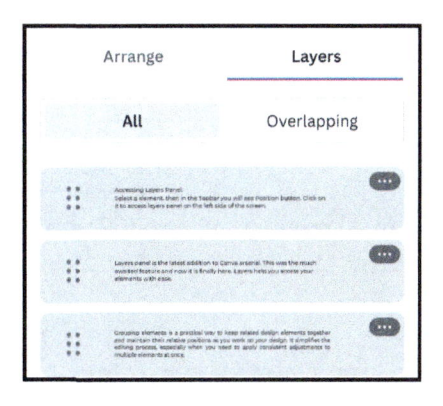

You will see 2 panels one all and other overlapping. All has all your layers. While overlapping will display only the layers that overlap each other.

Working with Layers Panel:
- To select any element on the canva just click on the layer and it will get selected.
- To move the layer up or down simply click on the layer and drag it.
- you can click on the 3 dots on top right of the layer to access more options such as copy, paste, duplicate, delete, layer, align, etc.
- To Delete a layer: Select the layer and Press Delete on your keyboard.
- Group elements will be displayed on one layer.

> Understanding how to work with layers in Canva allows you to have precise control over the arrangement and visibility of design elements. It's a fundamental skill for creating visually appealing and well-organized designs across a variety of projects.

CHOOSING TEMPLATES AND CUSTOMIZING DESIGNS

Canva offers a wide range of templates that can be used as a starting point for your designs. In this chapter, we will explore the process of choosing a template and customizing it to fit your needs.

Choosing a template:

To access Canva's templates, click on the "Templates" option in the left-hand menu.

You will see a list of templates organized by category, such as social media graphics, presentations, invitations, and more.

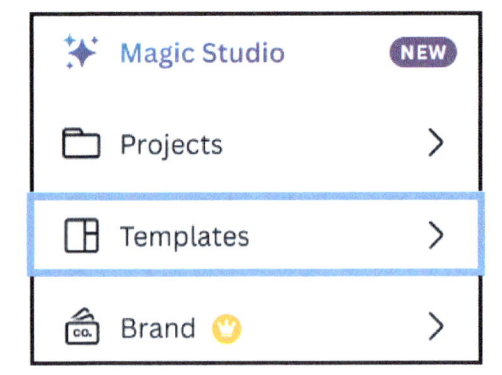

Browse through the templates and choose one that best fits your design needs.

Click on the template to open it in the Canva editor.

Customizing a template:

Once you have opened a template in the Canva editor, you can start customizing it to fit your needs.

You can change the text by clicking on it and typing in your own content.

You can also change the images by clicking on an image and selecting a new one from Canva's library or by uploading your own.

The toolbar at the left of the screen has options for adding design elements, such as shapes, lines, and icons.

You can also resize and rearrange elements within the design to create your desired layout.

> In conclusion, Canva's templates are a great starting point for your designs, and the platform makes it easy to customize templates to fit your needs. By using templates and customizing them, you can create professional-looking designs in no time.

CUSTOMIZING TEMPLATE

Once you have opened a template in the Canva editor, you can start customizing it to fit your needs.

You can change the text by clicking on it and typing in your own content.

You can also change the images by clicking on an image and selecting a new one from Canva's library or by uploading your own.

The toolbar at the left of the screen has options for adding design elements, such as shapes, lines, and icons.

You can also resize and rearrange elements within the design to create your desired layout.

Before    After

In conclusion, Canva's templates are a great starting point for your designs, and the platform makes it easy to customize templates to fit your needs. By using templates and customizing them, you can create professional-looking designs in no time.

CUSTOMIZING TEMPLATE

Now lets Customize this template into a more custom template

First delete the top left triangle, Bottom right black box

Move the right black box below the image.

Move the text design in front of graphic text.
Change color to Blue
Change the text Agency to Workshop and move it between graphic design

Change the Body text to Do you want to upscale your graphic design skills. Below this add

ONLINE WORKSHOP
30 SEPTEMBER
8AM - 12PM

69

CUSTOMIZING TEMPLATE

- Change learn more text to Register NOW and make it bold
- Change Contact us to Contact us for more information.
- Go to elements tab and type in Phone in the search bar. Click on the phone icon. Then resize and position it

Select orange elements and change them to blue color

- Go to elements tab and type in Instagram, YouTube, Twitter and Facebook respectively. Add respective icons below the Contact us bar. Then resize and position it

- Finally drag you image above the image
- adjust size and position of text and image
- delete any other elements or text

Editing any template is really easy in Canva. You can use it as a starting point and then customize it as per your requirements.

Instagram Post Designs

CREATING INSTAGRAM POST IN 5 STEPS

Here I will show how to create a Simple Instagram post design. This is a step by step tutorial that will help you create professional Instagram post design.

1. Start by adding the background.
Select the Square shape and size and place it as shown.
Color is #6f362a

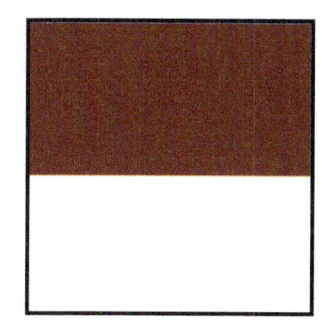

2. Go to elements tab, scroll down to frames and select the frame as shown in the image. Place it as shown

3. Add your photo. Click on the photo that you have uploaded in Upload tabs. It will be placed on the design, then simply drag and drop the image in the frame

4. Add Headline as
   "New style to make your decor modern"
   Font: Canva Sans size: 50 Color: #4b2913

   Add body text,
   Here I added just a placeholder text.
   Font: Montserrat size: 15 Color: #281618

CREATING INSTAGRAM POST

5. Add Text Shop NOW
   Font: Canva Sans size: 39 Color: #FFFFFF
   Select the text and click on Effect on the top bar

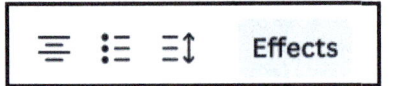

Select background and add the following values, Color #6f362a

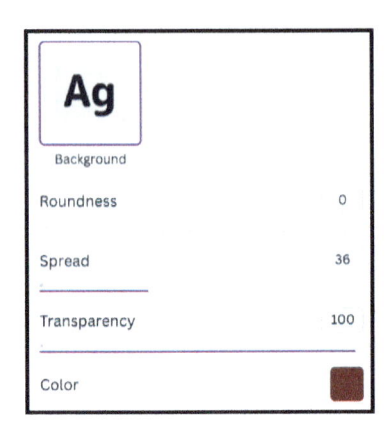

And all Done. Instagram post ready in 5 steps!

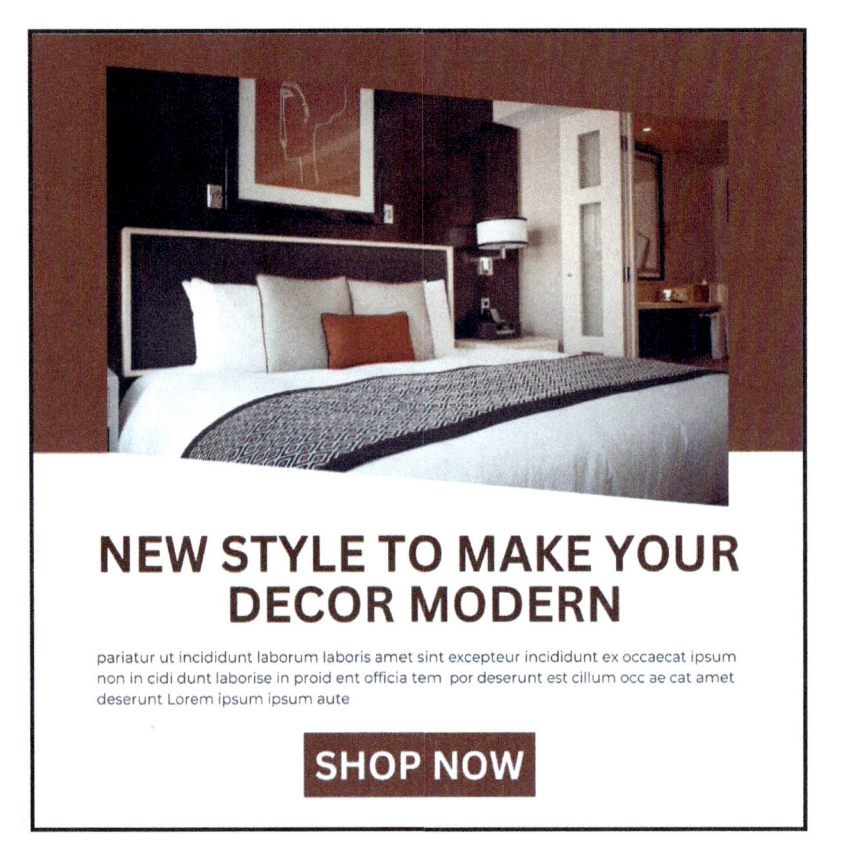

NEW STYLE TO MAKE YOUR DECOR MODERN

pariatur ut incididunt laborum laboris amet sint excepteur incididunt ex occaecat ipsum non in cidi dunt laborise in proid ent officia tem por deserunt est cillum occ ae cat amet deserunt Lorem ipsum ipsum aute

SHOP NOW

CREATING INSTAGRAM POST FOR PIZZA

Here I will show how to create a Pizza Instagram post design. This is a step by step tutorial that will help you create professional Instagram post design.

1. Start by adding a gradient to the background. Select the background.
add #ab003e color then, click on the + color icon and select gradient and add the other color. So we have 2 colors #ab003e and #ff914d orange.
Select radial gradient.

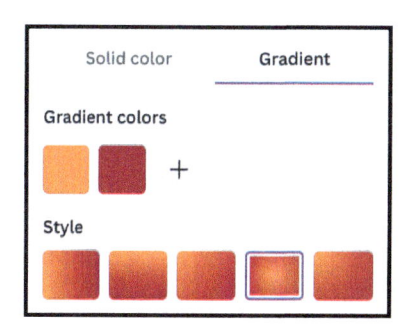

2. Go to elements tab and search Pizza. Then you will find these elements like tomato, mushroom, chilies. Add them to the background and place them as shown in the image. Reduce transparency to 17.

3. Add a isolated pizza photo. Then crop it in half. Simply double click on it and crop half part.

4. Add text with font Anton size for wait and it will be 66.4 and 116 for Gone and Pizza

74

CREATING INSTAGRAM POST FOR PIZZA

6. Now go to elements tab and search leaf, tomato, capsicum, chilly then add the respective element as shown in the image.
Now add a blur to the top left corner leaf by selecting the leaf and click on Edit Photo scroll down to blur and set the blur to 54, left chilly 61, top right tomato 50, capsicum 61.
Apply blur to all elements except the bottom tomato and right chilly.

7. Now add a rectangle shape to the top right. Go to elements tab and search home delivery, then add this element.
Write the text Free home delivery with font montessart size 13.6
Add a circle shape and place it as shown, Change color to #ab003e
add text 50% OFF font Anton size 42.8

8. Now add a rectangle shape to the bottom and change the color to #f67729.

9. Go to elements tab and search Instagram icon, Facebook icon, twitter icon, Pinterest icon. Then add and place it as shown in the image.

10. Go to elements tab and search Phone and add the element as shown in the image. Then add the text order Now and phone number with font Anton and size 32.8. Then add a line in between the social media icons and phone number, Color #ab003e

11. Lastly Go to elements tab and search arrow and place it as shown.

To download to Share button on top right and click on Download and select JPEG

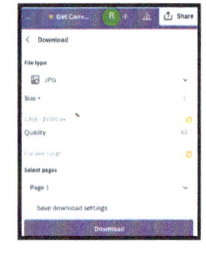

75

Text Animations

ANIMATION: TEXT ANIMATION

Animation makes design come to life, Animation in canva is a breeze.

How to animate text

Type in the text you want. Click on the Animate button on the top bar. you will see many animation options on the left panel of the screen.
There are 2 options Page Animation and Text Animation.
Click on Text Animation

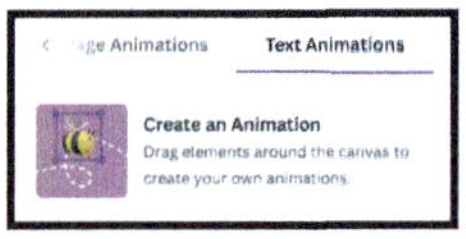

Basic animation

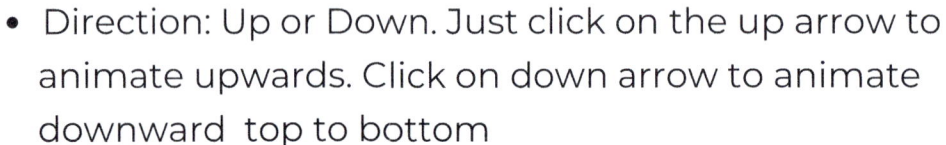

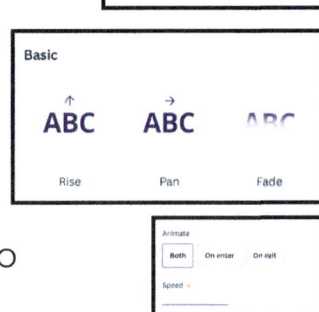

Rise: This will animate your text
Upwards from bottom to top.

- Speed: Just drag the slider to adjust the speed.
- Direction: Up or Down. Just click on the up arrow to animate upwards. Click on down arrow to animate downward top to bottom
- Animate: Both will animate on when animation starts and ends as well.
  On enter will animate only when the animation starts.
  On exit will animate only when the animation ends
- Reverse end animation: This will reverse direction of end animation. So if you have animation that goes up, if you check this it will go down.

Pan: This will animate your text left to right.

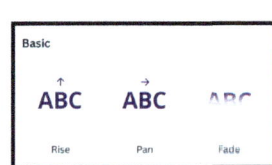

- Speed: Just drag the slider to adjust the speed.
- Direction: Left or Right. Just click on the Left arrow to animate Right to left. Click on Right arrow to animate left to right.
- Animate: Both will animate when animation starts and ends as well.
  On enter will animate only when the animation starts.
  On exit will animate only when the animation ends
- Reverse end animation: This will reverse direction of end animation. So if you have animation that goes left, if you check this it will go right.

ANIMATION: TEXT ANIMATION

Basic animation

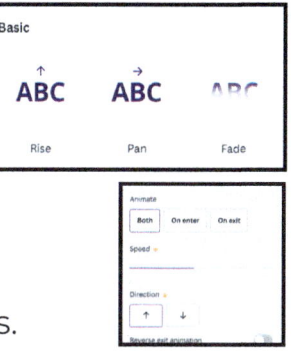

Fade: This will animate your text 0 opacity to 100% opacity.

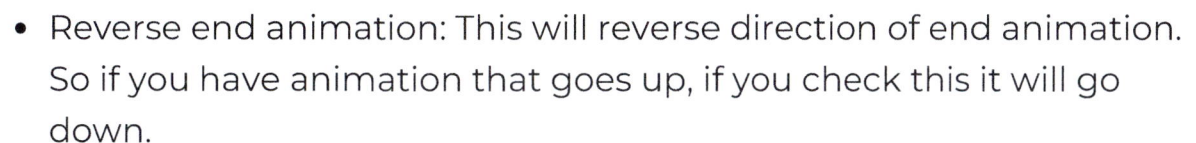

- Speed: Just drag the slider to adjust the speed.
- Animate: Both will animate on when animation starts and ends as well.
  On enter will animate only when the animation starts.
  On exit will animate only when the animation ends
- Reverse end animation: This will reverse direction of end animation. So if you have animation that goes up, if you check this it will go down.
- Writing Style: 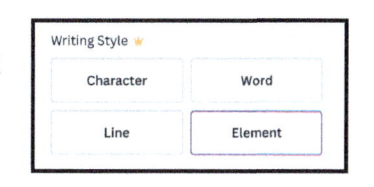
1. Character will fade in each character(letters) of text
2. Word will fade in each word of the text
3. line will fade in each of the text
4. Element will fade in entire text box as a whole

POP: This will animate your text as popping out to in. 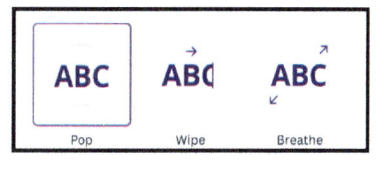
- Speed: Just drag the slider to adjust the speed
- Animate: Both will animate on when animation
- starts and ends as well.
  On enter will animate only when the animation starts.
  On exit will animate only when the animation ends

Wipe: This will animation text like it is wiping text left to right. 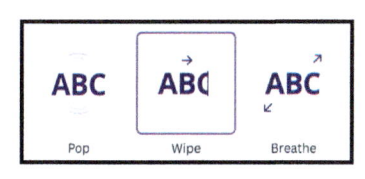
- Speed: Just drag the slider to adjust the speed
- Animate: Both will animate on when animation
- starts and ends as well.
  On enter will animate only when the animation starts.
  On exit will animate only when the animation ends
- Direction: You can change the direction of up, down, left or right

78

ANIMATION: TEXT ANIMATION

Basic animation

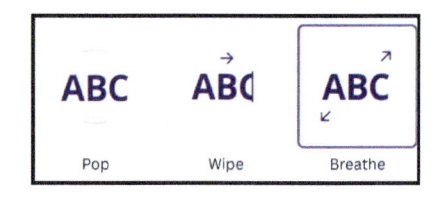

Breathe: This will animate your text slowly like breathing in to out.

- Scale: Just drag the slider to adjust the Scale.
- in/out: Click In to animate out to in,
  out will animate in to out.

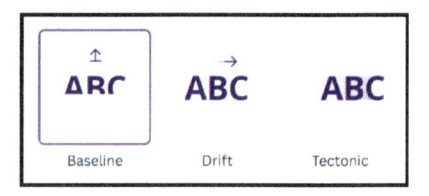

Baseline: This will animate your text like it is coming out from base

- Speed: Just drag the slider to adjust the speed
- Animate: Both will animate on when animation
- starts and ends as well.
  On enter will animate only when the animation starts.
  On exit will animate only when the animation ends
- Direction: You can change the direction of up, down, left or right

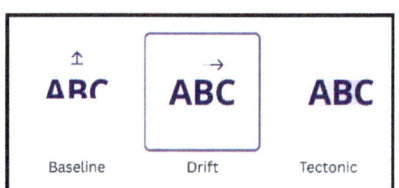

Drift: This will animate your text like drifting/moving little little in the direction selected.

- Intensity: Just drag the slider to adjust the speed
- Direction: You can change the direction of up, down, left or right

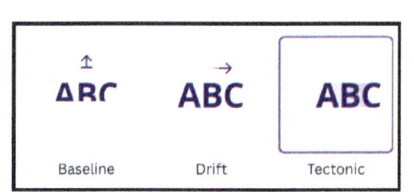

Tectonic: This will animate your text like tectonic little little in the direction selected.

- Intensity: Just drag the slider to adjust the speed

ANIMATION: TEXT ANIMATION

Writing animation

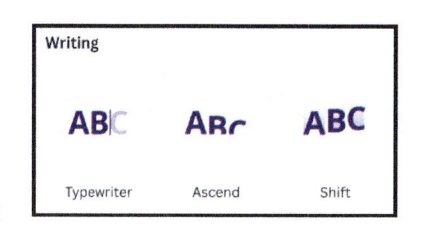

Typewriter: This will animate your text as typing
- Speed: Just drag the slider to adjust the speed
- Character/ Word: You can select character or word. Character will animate every letter, while word will animate every word

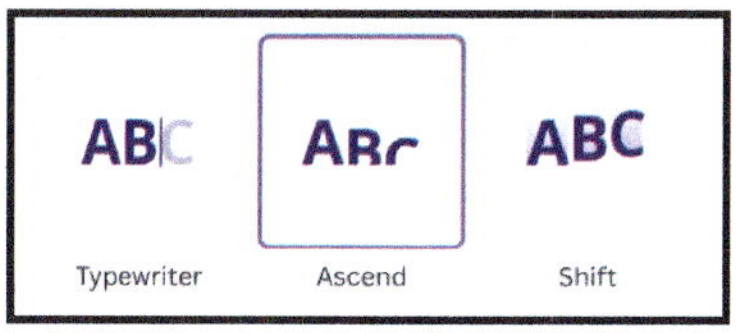

Ascend: This will move animate your text bottom to top
- Speed: Just drag the slider to adjust the speed
- word/ Line: You can select Line or word. word will animate every word, while line will animate every line
- Animate: Both will animate on when animation
- starts and ends as well.
  On enter will animate only when the animation starts.
  On exit will animate only when the animation ends
- Direction: You can change the direction of up, down, left or right

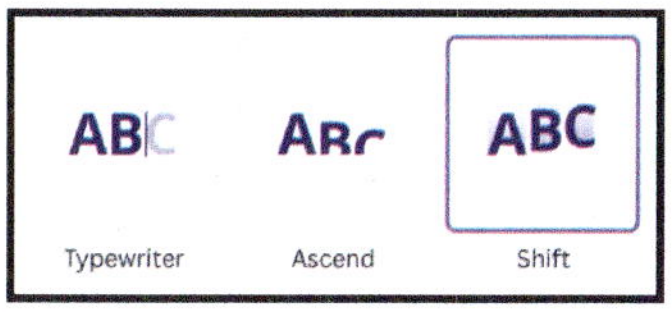

Shift: This will animate your text top to bottom or as the direction selected.
- Character/ Word/line: You can select character or word. Character will animate every letter, while word will animate every word, line will animate every line.
- Speed: Just drag the slider to adjust the speed
- Direction: You can change the direction of up, down, left or right

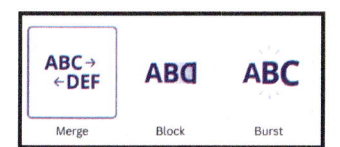

Merge: This is especially useful when you have 2 lines. so top line will animate to left and bottom to right.
- Intensity: Just drag the slider to adjust the speed

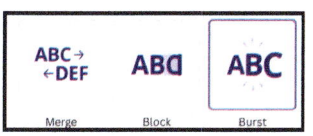

Burst: This will burst every letter creating a burst writing
- Intensity: Just drag the slider to adjust the speed

80

ANIMATION: TEXT ANIMATION

Writing animation

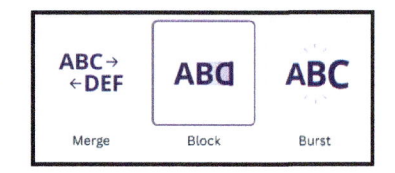

Block: This will animate a block over your text.
- Color: Set color of the block the will animate over your text.
- Animate: Both will animate on when animation starts and ends as well.
  On enter will animate only when the animation starts.
  On exit will animate only when the animation ends
- Direction: You can change the direction of up, down, left or right

Bounce: This will bounce animate your text from top to bottom
- Character/ Word: You can select character or word. Character will animate every letter, while word will animate every word.
- Animate: Both will animate on when animation starts and ends as well.
  On enter will animate only when the animation starts.
  On exit will animate only when the animation ends.
- Intensity: Just drag the slider to adjust the speed.

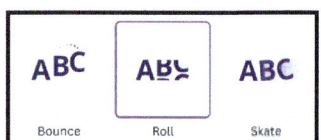

Roll: This will roll animate your text from top to bottom
- Character/ Word/Line/Element: You can select character or word. Character will animate every letter, while word will animate every word. Line will animate each line. Element will animate each text block.

Skate: This will animate your text as skating from left to right or vice versa as selected.
- Animate: Both will animate on when animation starts and ends as well. On enter will animate only when the animation starts. On exit will animate only when the animation ends.
- Intensity: Just drag the slider to adjust the speed.

ANIMATION: TEXT ANIMATION

Writing animation

Spread: This will spread your text out or in

- Scale: Set the amount of scale of spread
- Animate: Both will animate on when animation starts and ends as well.
  On enter will animate only when the animation starts.
  On exit will animate only when the animation ends
- In/Out: In will spread text in from out to in and out will spread text in to out.

ANIMATION: TEXT ANIMATION

Exaggerate animation

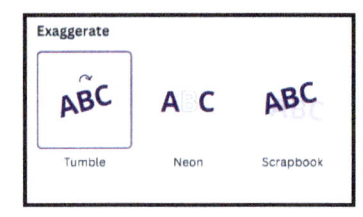

Tumble: This will tumble your text from left out of the screen to the place of text.
- Animate: Both will animate on when animation starts and ends as well.
  On enter will animate only when the animation starts.
  On exit will animate only when the animation ends
- Intensity: Just drag the slider to adjust the intensity of animation

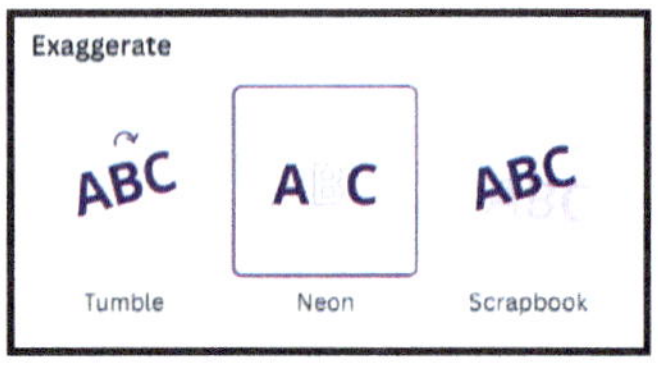

Neon: This will animate your text as neon lights.
- Animate: Both will animate on when animation starts and ends as well.
  On enter will animate only when the animation starts.
  On exit will animate only when the animation ends
- Intensity: Just drag the slider to adjust the intensity of animation
- Character/ Word/Line/Element: You can select character, word, text or element. Character will animate every letter, while word will animate every word. Line will animate each line. Element will animate each text block.

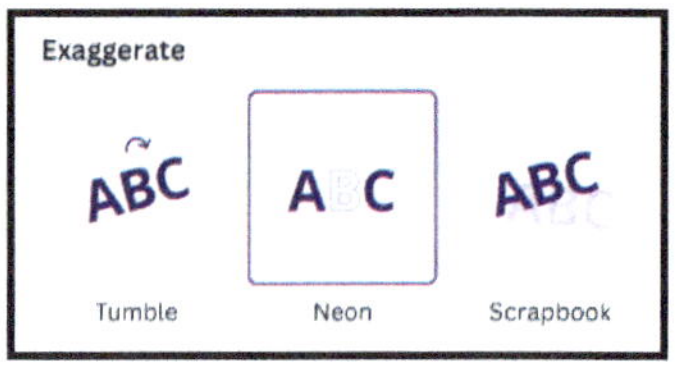

Scrapbook: This will animate your text in scrapbook style from left out of the screen to the place of text.
- Animate: Both will animate on when animation starts and ends as well.
  On enter will animate only when the animation starts.
  On exit will animate only when the animation ends

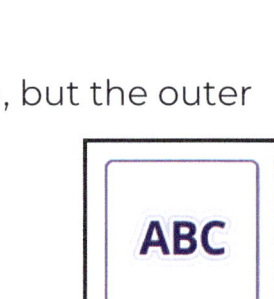

Stomp: This will animate your text from out of screen to in, but the outer text is gigantic. So it looks like a stomp!
- Animate: Both will animate on when animation starts and ends as well.
  On enter will animate only when the animation starts.
  On exit will animate only when the animation ends

ANIMATION: TEXT ANIMATION

Add motion effects

These effects are added above all the text animations discussed earlier. For example you add typing text animation and you apply this motion effect of pulse. There will be typing and pulse animation.

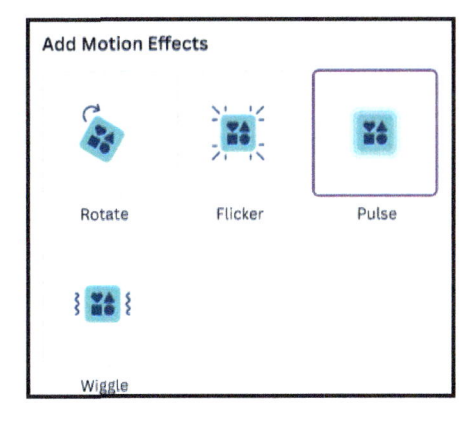

Rotate: This will rotate your text clockwise or counter clockwise.

Flicker: This will flicker your text like reduce opacity and increase it.

Pulse: This will effect is like heart beat effect. Pulsing in and out

wiggle: This will effect will literally wiggle your text.

Animations

ANIMATION

This is the latest mind blowing feature added in Canva. This is so simple and effective way to animate anything.

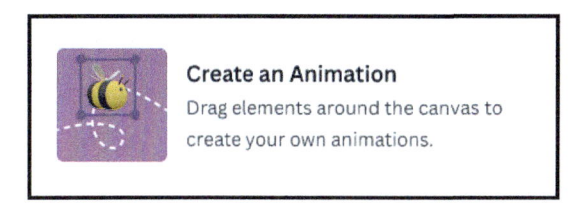

Create an Animation
Drag elements around the canvas to create your own animations.

How to animate:

This is so simple, just select your text or element and start dragging it like you want to animate! all done your animation is ready!
isn't it mind blowing

After you drag and leave you will these options

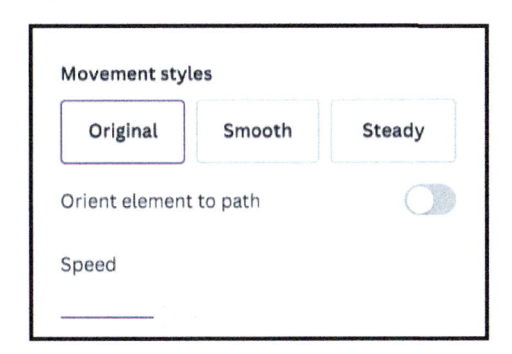

Movement styles: Original, Smooth, Steady
Orient element to path
Speed

Select and drag an element around the canvas to create your animation.

Tips
- Hold shift whilst dragging to create straight lines.
- Control the speed of your animation by moving the element faster or slower.
- Stop dragging the element to complete your animation.

Smooth: Will smooth the animation.
Steady: This will make your animation steady over the course of animation.

Orient element to path: This will make your element face the direction of path

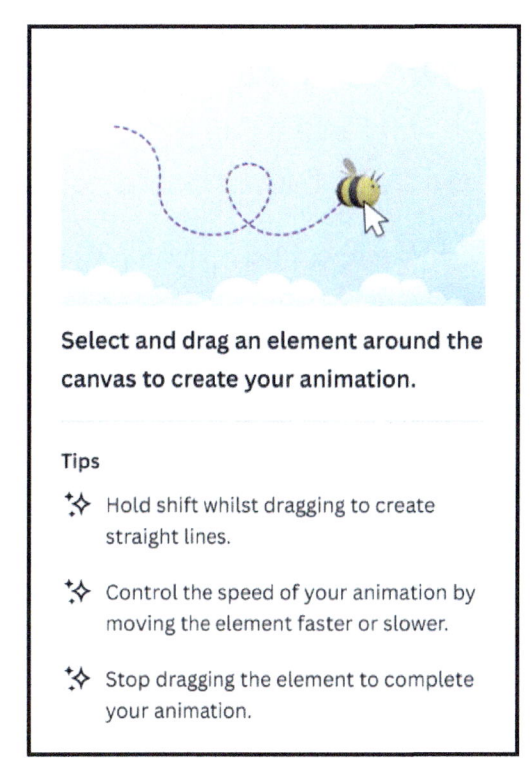

Speed: Just drag the slider to increase or decrease the speed of animation.

PAGE ANIMATION

Page animation will animate all the elements on page. These are similar to text animation but here all the elements on the page will be animated.

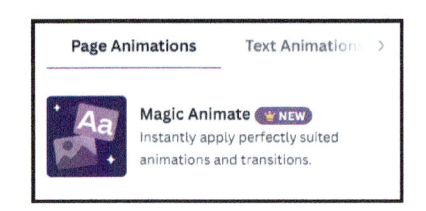

Magic Animate: This is the latest animation added to Canva magic design. This will automatically apply page animation that will best suit your page content.

Combination

Simple : This will apply a simple animation that will fade in all the element one after other from top to bottom.

Sleek: This will apply a rise animation that will bring in all the element one after other from bottom to top. This also applies skate text animation to heading.

Fun: This will bring in all the element one after other from top to bottom slightly overlapping one another creating interesting effect.

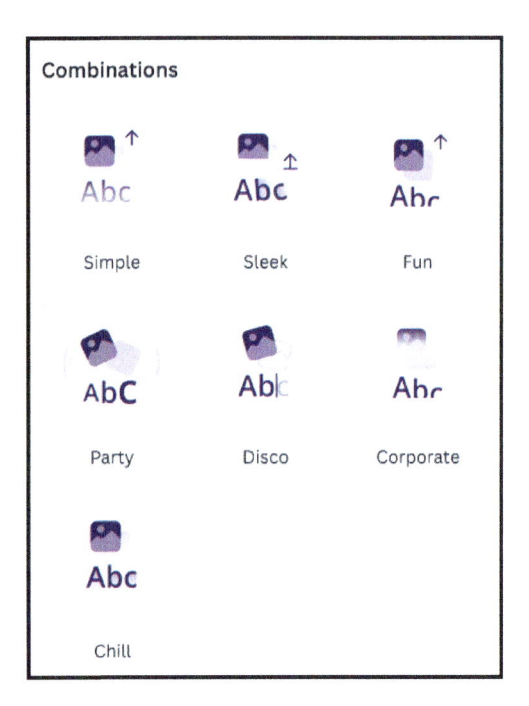

Party: This will bring in all the element one after other from left of screen on to the page creating interesting effect. Text will also be applied a bounce animation

Disco: Text will be applied a typewriter animation while images will have neon effect.

Corporate: Text will be applied a Ascend animation while images will have no effect.

Chill: Text will be applied a Fade animation while images will have also have fade effect. All elements will face in from top to bottom one by one.

PAGE ANIMATION

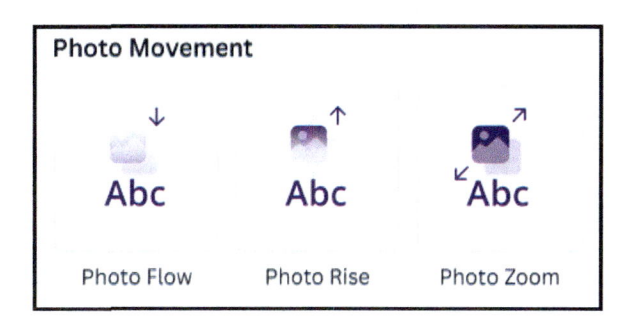

Photo Movement:

- Photo Flow: This will apply a fade animation to all the elements from top to bottom one by one. So elements will fade in one by one starting from top element to the bottom sequentially.
- Photo Rise: This will fade in elements from bottom to top sequentially .
- Photo Zoom: Will Zoom in photo on the page so they will go from high scale and lower scale.

Audio And Video

ADDING AND EDITING VIDEOS

In today's multimedia-rich digital landscape, incorporating video into your designs can bring a dynamic and engaging dimension to your creations. In this chapter, we will explore how to seamlessly integrate videos into your Canva designs and take advantage of various multimedia options to create captivating visual content.

To add video go to the elements tab > scroll down to videos and click on see all.

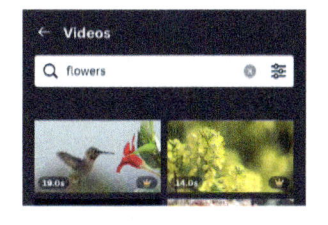

To find the video you want, type in the search bar.

Just click on the video and it will be added to the canvas. You have many options to edit the video on the top bar.

Edit video: The most amazing feature of background removal, this is a pro feature only.
Secondly this lets you apply filters to your video, these are free to use.

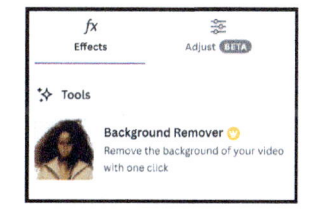

Cut/Trim: You can also cut your video using this cut feature. You'll notice handles (small squares) on the edges of the video. Drag the handles inwards to trim the video from the beginning or end, depending on the portion you want to keep.

ADDING AND EDITING VIDEOS

Playback: With this you can adjust the speed of video. You can increase or decrease the speed of video. You can also make it loop by just turning on the slider button. And Auto play in presentation will play your video as soon as it come on the presentation slide. You can turn it off, then you have to manually play it in presentation.

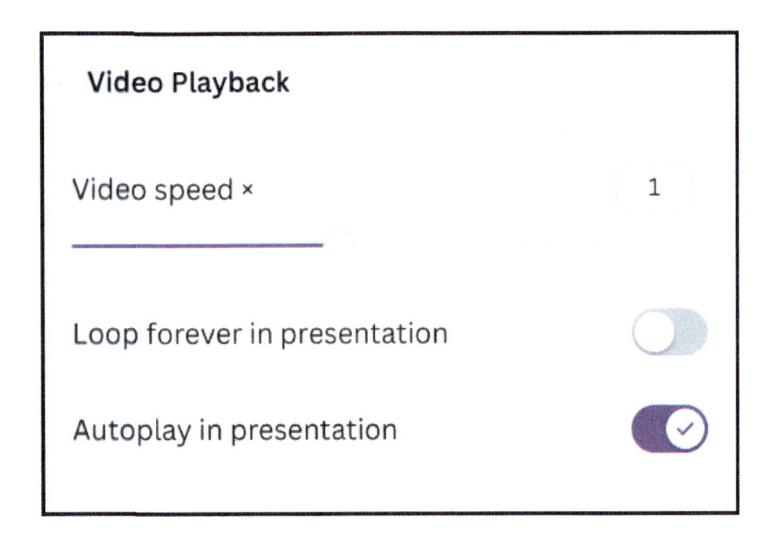

Volume: let you control the volume. 100 to 0.

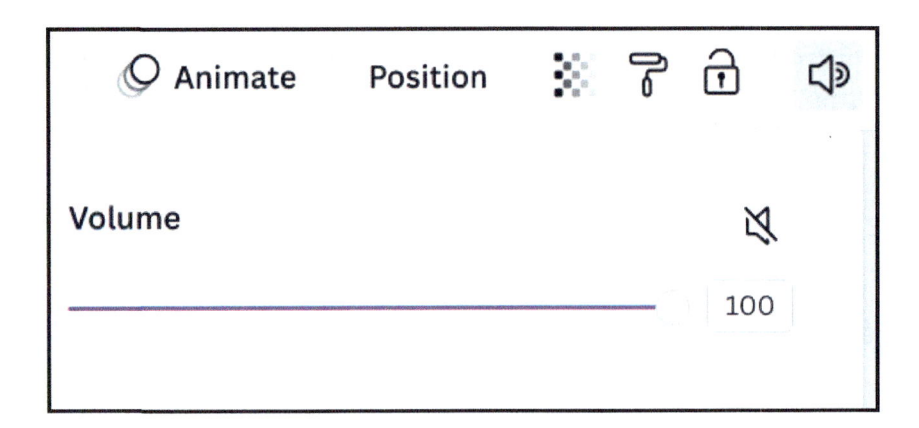

ADDING AND EDITING AUDIO

Adding Background Music

Access Audio Elements: Click on the "Elements" tab from the left side of screen

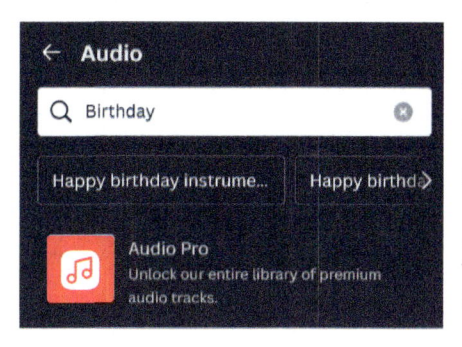

Select "Audio: Browse Canva's audio library or upload your own music track. Type in the search that you want.

Just click on the audio you want and it will be added to your design.

Adjusting Audio Duration and Position

Tailor the audio to match the timing and content of your design: Trimming Audio: Click on the audio in the timeline to select it.

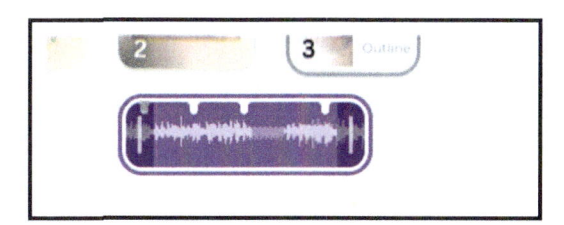

Handles: Drag the handles at the edges of the audio element to trim its duration.

Positioning: Move the audio element along the timeline to align with specific portions of your design.

ADDING AND EDITING AUDIO

Adjusting Volume and Muting

Control the audio's presence and volume within your design:
1. Muting Audio: Click on the audio in the timeline to select it.
2. Mute Option: In the editor panel on top of the canvas, use the "Mute" toggle to turn off the audio if needed.

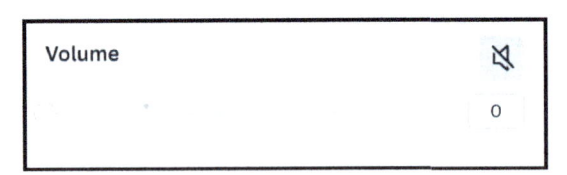

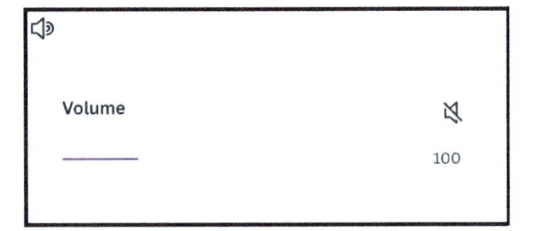

3. Volume Control: Adjust the volume using the volume slider in the editor panel.

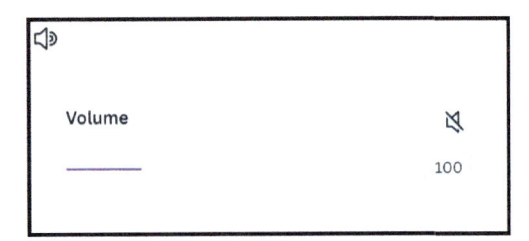

Adjust: You can adjust the audio to match specific part without cutting/ moving the entire clip. It is useful when you have a large audio file.
1. Select the audio in timeline
2. Then click on Adjust on top bar of canvas.

Now simply drag the audio file in the time to set the position.

Beat Sync: This is a Pro feature. It will automatically sync your audio with video clips.

93

ADDING AND EDITING AUDIO

Using Sound Effects

Sound effects can enhance specific moments in your designs:
Explore Sound Effects: Click on the "Elements" tab and select "Sound effects" to explore Canva's library.

- Adding Sound Effects: Just click the chosen sound effect and it will be added to the canvas.
- Timing: Adjust the timing and position of the sound effect in the timeline.

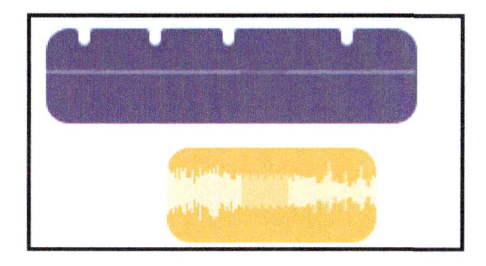

Exporting Design with Audio

Once your design is complete with audio, you can export and share it:
- Click on Share button on the top right of the screen then click the "Download" button.
- Choose Format: Select the format MP4 that includes the audio.
- Share and Publish: Share your design on social media, websites, presentations, and more.

Maintaining a Balanced Audio Experience

Keep the audio experience balanced and harmonious:
- Consider the Message: Ensure that the chosen audio elements align with the message and tone of your design.
- Subtlety: Background music should complement the design without overpowering other elements. So keep the volume to the appropriate level.

By incorporating audio elements thoughtfully, you can create designs that not only capture the eye but also engage the ears, resulting in a richer and more memorable experience for your audience.

Canva AI
And
New Features

DRAW

The latest addition to Canva new feature is Draw. Now you can draw freehand using the "Draw" tool to create custom illustrations, doodles, or handwritten text.

On the left side of the Canva interface, you'll typically find a "Draw" tool. Click on it to activate the freehand drawing feature.

And you will get all these pencil, pen and marker.

All you have to do is select any one of these and start drawing! As simple as that.

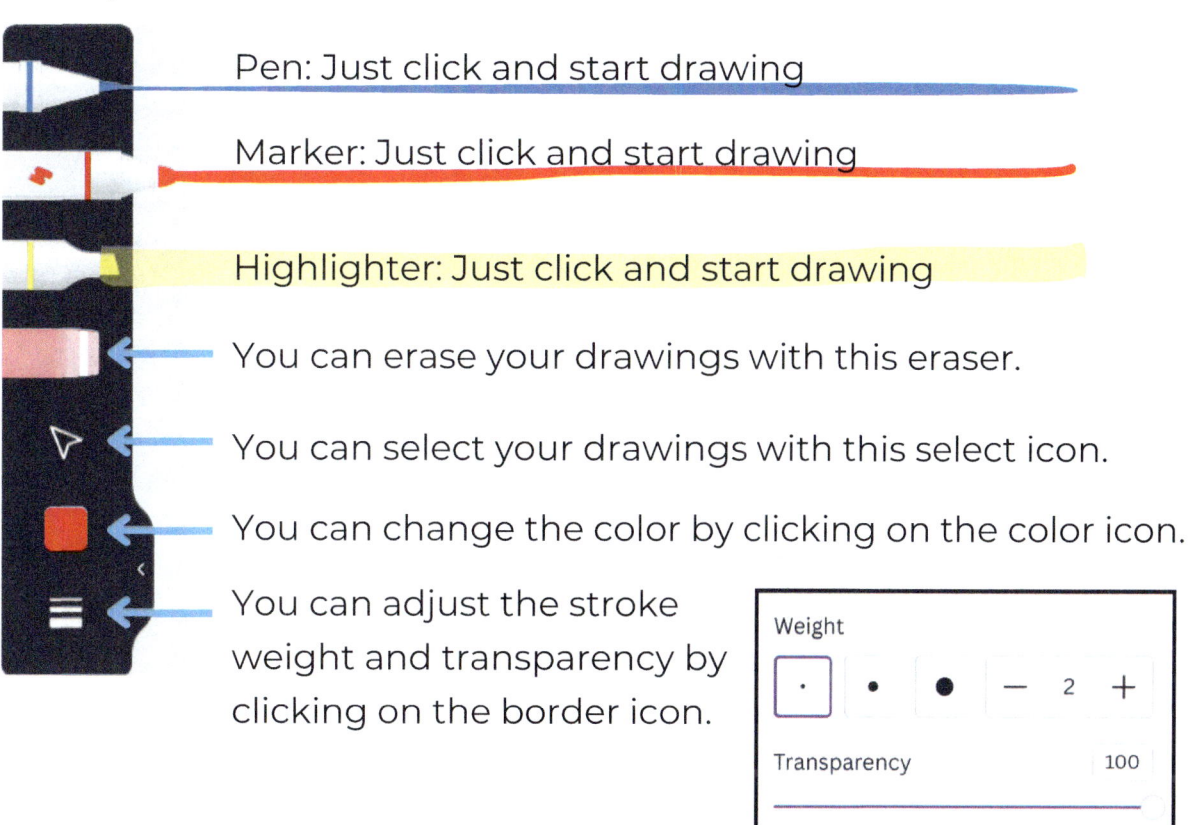

Pen: Just click and start drawing

Marker: Just click and start drawing

Highlighter: Just click and start drawing

You can erase your drawings with this eraser.

You can select your drawings with this select icon.

You can change the color by clicking on the color icon.

You can adjust the stroke weight and transparency by clicking on the border icon.

Using the "Draw" tool in Canva allows you to add a personal and creative touch to your designs. Whether it's custom illustrations, handwritten notes, or unique doodles, this tool empowers you to add your artistic flair to your projects.

MAGIC WRITE

This is the new Magical feature added to Canva. As the name suggest it helps you write magically just by giving the title! Canva AI feature

There are many ways to access it.

1. Click on the text box and you get this option Magic Write on top of it.

   ✨ Magic Write

2. From the Canva Assistant that is the round icon with stars on the right bottom of screen.

3. In Canva docs.

How to use:

1. Click on the text box and you get this option Magic Write on top of it: Now you can click on any of these options. So it will add to your text, summarize it, rewrite it, make it fun or formal or it will sprinkle fairy dust to it!
You can also choose to fix spellings.

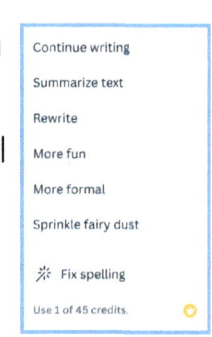

   - Continue writing
   - Summarize text
   - Rewrite
   - More fun
   - More formal
   - Sprinkle fairy dust
   - Fix spelling
   - Use 1 of 45 credits.

2. From the Canva Assistant that is the round icon with stars on the right bottom of screen:
Click on it and select Magic write, Then enter in the text you want to generate. Enter a line about what text you want to generate.

   ✏️ Magic Write™   ✕
   Use 5 or more words to describe what you want to   ✨ Try an example

   ⓘ Use 1 of 44 credits. Upgrade for more.   **Generate**   Ctrl+Enter
   Part of Magic Studio⁺

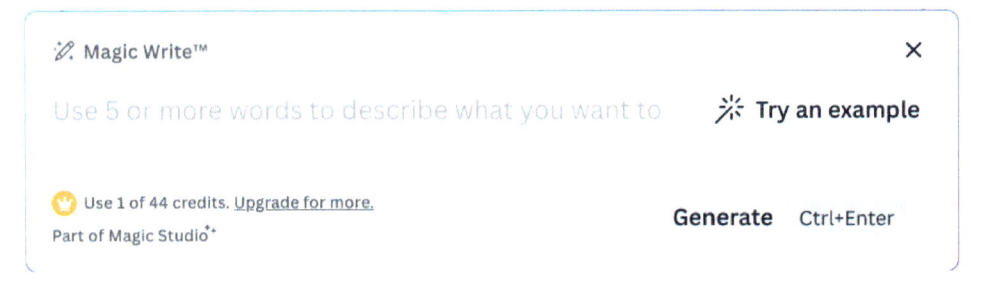

If you select a text and click on it then you will get the same options as above no 1.

> Magic write is a AI powered feature that heps you write any content with ease. You don't have to be a expert writer. You can also use it to brainstorm ideas, write blog, post, articles, or just about anything.

MAGIC WRITE

3. In Canva docs:

Click on the + icon and select magic write. You will get a pop up where you need to enter the text that you want to write. Example:

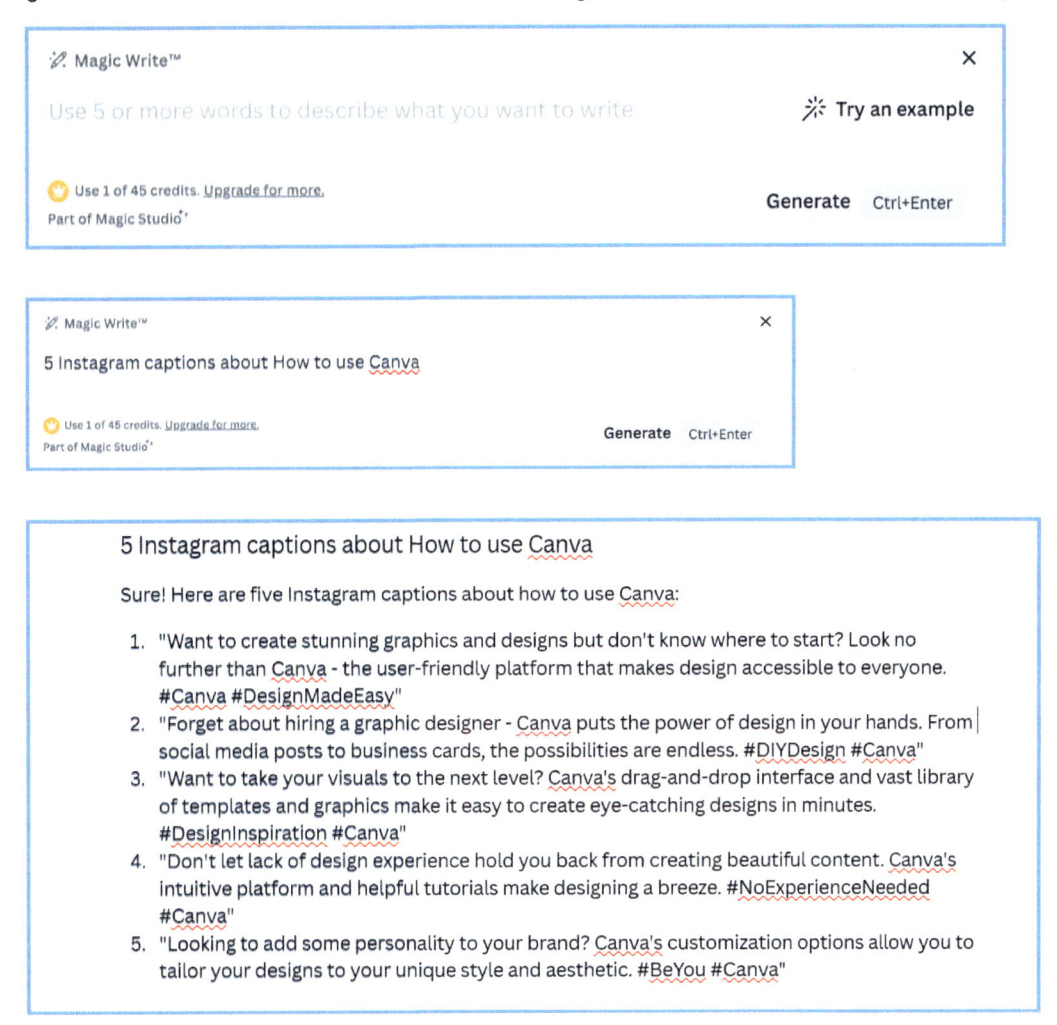

Magic Write™

Use 5 or more words to describe what you want to write — Try an example

Use 1 of 45 credits. Upgrade for more.
Part of Magic Studio

Generate   Ctrl+Enter

Magic Write™

5 Instagram captions about How to use Canva

Use 1 of 45 credits. Upgrade for more.
Part of Magic Studio

Generate   Ctrl+Enter

---

5 Instagram captions about How to use Canva

Sure! Here are five Instagram captions about how to use Canva:

1. "Want to create stunning graphics and designs but don't know where to start? Look no further than Canva - the user-friendly platform that makes design accessible to everyone. #Canva #DesignMadeEasy"
2. "Forget about hiring a graphic designer - Canva puts the power of design in your hands. From social media posts to business cards, the possibilities are endless. #DIYDesign #Canva"
3. "Want to take your visuals to the next level? Canva's drag-and-drop interface and vast library of templates and graphics make it easy to create eye-catching designs in minutes. #DesignInspiration #Canva"
4. "Don't let lack of design experience hold you back from creating beautiful content. Canva's intuitive platform and helpful tutorials make designing a breeze. #NoExperienceNeeded #Canva"
5. "Looking to add some personality to your brand? Canva's customization options allow you to tailor your designs to your unique style and aesthetic. #BeYou #Canva"

Magic write is a AI powered feature that helps you write any content with ease. You don't have to be a expert writer. You can also use it to brainstorm ideas, write blog, post, articles, or just about anything.

DOCS

Docs are latest and greatest addition to Canva. You can create awesome documents using Canva Docs.

How to access

From the home screen click on docs Icon and select Document

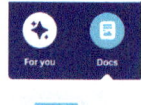

Now you have a document.

Start typing in your text.

Click on the + icon and you will get many options

- Heading: Click on it to add a Headline, So it will have font size and style of heading.
- Subheading: Click on it to add a Subheading, So it will have font size and style of Subheading.
- Body: Click on it to add a Body text, So it will have font size and style of Body text.
- Table: You can add a table. You can edit it as per the lesson in the earlier lesson.
- Checklist: With this you can add a checklist. When you click on the box it add a check mark in the box. 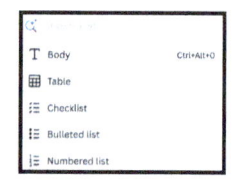
- Bullet list: With this you can add a bullet list.
- Numbered List: This will add a numbered list.
- Pie Chart: You can add a pie chart. just fill in the data on the left of the screen and you will have your chart ready.
- Bar Chart: You can add a bar chart. just fill in the data on the left of the screen and you will have your chart ready. 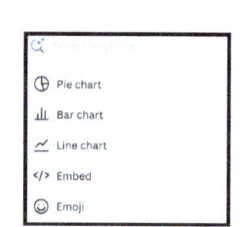
- Line Chart: You can add a line chart. just fill in the data on the left of the screen and you will have your chart ready.
- Embed: you can embed documents, videos here. just paste in the embed link
- Emoji: You can add emoji, There are many. just click on the one you want.

DOCS

- Magic Write: This is an awesome AI Canva feature. Just Click on magic write. Then describe what you want to generate written and it will be generated in just a click!
- Design: with this you can a banner, when you click on it, it will open some templates that you can use. Simply edit it as per your requirements. Change text, colors and images.

Templates

- Click on the templates tab from the left of the screen.
  You will get all the templates that you can use as doc template.
- you can also search for any template you want by typing in the search bar. Editing template is as simple as changing text, colors and images.

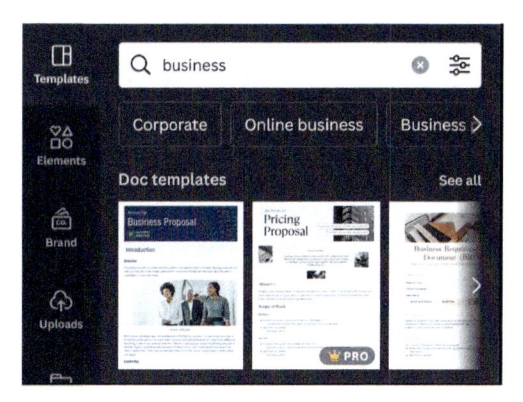

Canva Docs makes it easy to create documents that not only convey information but also make them visually appealing.

MAGIC EDIT

This is yet another Canva AI feature that will just blow your mind. You can edit photo to change anything in the photo by just entering the text!

Select the Photo you want to edit

Click on Edit Photo from the topbar.

Select Magic Edit from the left side of the screen.

Brush over the photo the you want to change or edit and click on Continue

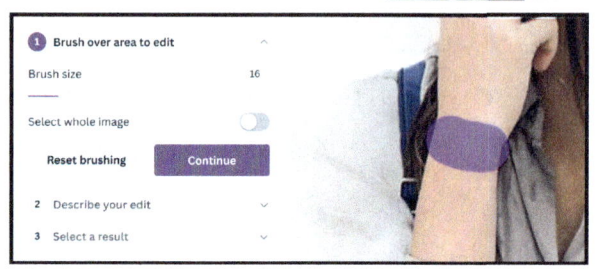

Then enter in what you want the results to be. and click on generate

You will get multiple options. select the one that you like and click on Done.

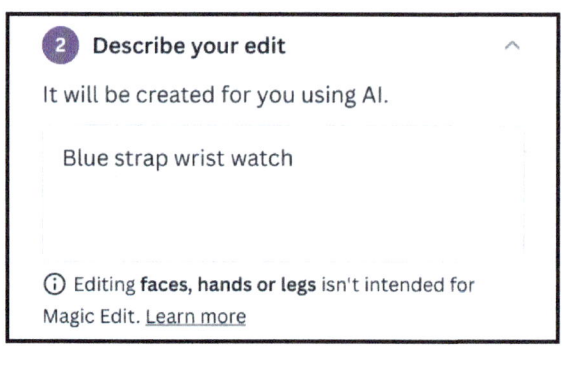

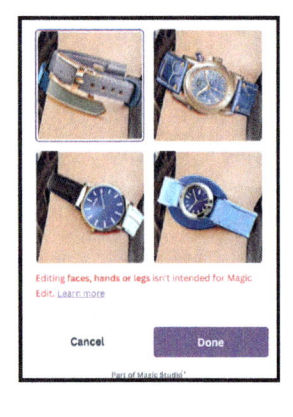

Magic Edit is a cutting-edge AI-powered tool that revolutionizes image generation and editing, enabling you to elevate your photos to entirely new heights.

MAGIC EDIT

This is yet another Canva AI feature that will just blow your mind. You can edit photo to change anything in the photo by just entering the text!

Select the Photo you want to edit

Click on Edit Photo from the topbar.

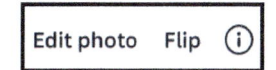

Select Magic Edit from the left side of the screen.

Brush over the photo the you want to change or edit and click on Continue

Then enter in what you want the results to be. and click on generate

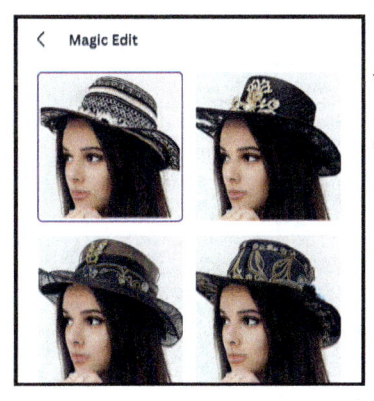

You will get multiple options. select the one that you like and click on Done.

Magic Edit is a cutting-edge AI-powered tool that revolutionizes image generation and editing, enabling you to elevate your photos to entirely new heights.

MAGIC MEDIA

This is yet another Canva AI feature that will just blow your mind. You can generate any image just entering the text!

How to use:
Go to apps tab from the left bar of the screen.
Select Magic media

Now simply type in the text that you want to generate. include colors, places, movement, etc.

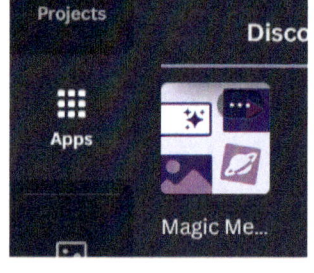

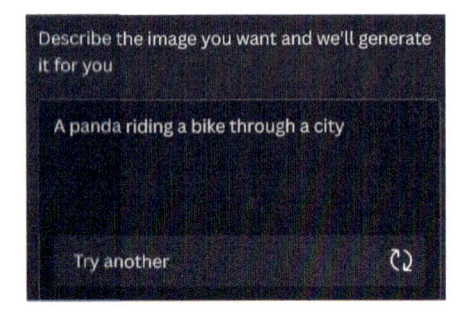

Select the style you want. There are many to choose from filmic, watercolor, photo, dreamy and anime.

Select the aspect ratio. and click on Generate.

It will generate 4 options. Click on the image and it will add to the canvas

Magic Edit is a cutting-edge AI-powered tool that revolutionizes image generation and editing, enabling you to elevate your photos to entirely new heights.

KEYBOARD SHORTCUTS

Keyboard shortcuts in Canva can significantly speed up your design workflow and make your editing and design tasks more efficient. Here are some commonly used keyboard shortcuts in Canva:

Basic Editing Shortcuts:
1. Copy selected elements: Ctrl (Windows) / Command (Mac) + C
2. Cut selected elements: Ctrl (Windows) / Command (Mac) + X
3. Paste copied or cut elements: Ctrl (Windows) / Command (Mac) + V
4. Undo your last action: Ctrl (Windows) / Command (Mac) + Z
5. Redo your last action: Ctrl (Windows) / Command (Mac) + Shift + Z

Element Selection Shortcuts:
1. Select all elements on the canvas: Ctrl (Windows) / Command (Mac) + A
2. Tab: Cycle through elements in the current group.

Duplicate elements Shortcuts:
1. Duplicate selected elements :
Ctrl (Windows) / Command (Mac) + D

Grouping and Ungrouping Shortcuts:
1. Group selected elements: Ctrl (Windows) / Command (Mac) + G
2. Ungroup selected elements: Ctrl (Windows) / Command (Mac) + Shift + G

Layer arrangement Shortcuts:
1. Send selected elements backward one layer:
Ctrl (Windows) / Command (Mac) + [
2. Bring selected elements forward one layer:
Ctrl (Windows) / Command (Mac) +]
3. Send selected elements to the back:
Ctrl (Windows) / Command (Mac) + Shift + [
4. Bring selected elements to the front:
Ctrl (Windows) / Command (Mac) + Shift +]

> These keyboard shortcuts can enhance your productivity when working in Canva by allowing you to perform tasks more quickly.

KEYBOARD SHORTCUTS

Text Editing Shortcuts:
1. Bold text: Ctrl (Windows) / Command (Mac) + B
2. Italicize text: Ctrl (Windows) / Command (Mac) + I
3. Underline text: Ctrl (Windows) / Command (Mac) + U
4. Increase font size: Ctrl (Windows) / Command (Mac) + Shift + >
5. Decrease font size: Ctrl (Windows) / Command (Mac) + Shift + <
6. Add a text box: T
7. Convert text to uppercase: Ctrl (Windows) / Command (Mac) + Shift + K

Canvas Navigation Shortcuts:
1. Zoom in on the canvas: Ctrl (Windows) / Command (Mac) + +
2. Zoom out on the canvas: Ctrl (Windows) / Command (Mac) + -
3. Fit the canvas to the screen: Ctrl (Windows) / Command (Mac) + 0

Start Searching: /

These shortcuts can be incredibly handy when you're working on various design projects in Canva. They help you perform tasks more efficiently and navigate the platform with ease. Feel free to experiment with these keyboard shortcuts to find the ones that work best for your specific design needs.

USEFUL LINKS

Follow me

- @Designmywebworld

- @pooja-awasthi31

- @Designmywebworld   Canva Tutorials, tips and tricks

- @Designmywebworld

- @IReallyCreative

Website

https://Designmywebworld.my.canva.site/

Email

If you need help with Canva or graphic design please feel free to contact me

poojathegrapicdesigner@gmail.com

Follow me to learn more bout canva tutorials, tips and tricks. be updated with Latest Canva features. We can also Connect, share and collaborate on design projects.

Printed in Great Britain
by Amazon